# Paranormal

# Purbeck

## *A Study of the Unexplained*

David Leadbetter

Roving
Press

© 2013 David Leadbetter

Published by Roving Press Ltd
4 Southover Cottages, Frampton, Dorset, DT2 9NQ, UK
Tel: +44 (0)1300 321531
www.rovingpress.co.uk

Whilst every care has been taken in the production of this publication, no liability can be accepted for any errors or omissions. Please contact the publisher if you find any, and we will try to rectify at next printing. The author has endeavoured to cite clear locations, though where a private address is involved the name of the road is often just given for privacy and it should be emphasised that readers should not attempt to call on someone's family home.

First published 2013 by Roving Press Ltd

ISBN: 978-1-906651-220


British Library Cataloguing in Publication Data
A catalogue record for this book is available from the British Library

Cover design by Tim Musk. Front photograph by Anna Ivanova (© iStockphoto.com/Anna Ivanova), back photograph by Matt Gibson (©iStockphoto.com/Matt Gibson)

Set in 11.5/13 pt Minion Pro by Beamreach Printing (www.beamreachuk.co.uk)
Printed and bound by Henry Ling Ltd, at the Dorset Press, Dorchester, DT1 1HD

# Contents

# Acknowledgements

Over 100 people have contributed accounts of either their own personal experiences or those of others to this book, and a list of contributors now follows, with apologies to any whose names may have inadvertently been omitted. Two people in particular deserve special mention: they are publican Rachael Aplin and local historian Reg Saville. Rachael gave me unrestricted access to the Royal Oak at Herston, Swanage, and provided many useful contacts, while Reg sent a lot of interesting material relating to Langton Matravers. Without their help this book would have been considerably slimmer! Throughout I have endeavoured to transcribe the various accounts as faithfully as possible, in some cases preserving the person's original words. The photography is mostly my own, apart from the photo of Phil Murray and one of myself taken by Mo Murray (who also inspired the front cover image), Rachael Aplin in the Royal Oak garden supplied by Martin Curtis, and orbs in the same garden taken by Lil Hosegood. I thank David Haysom at Swanage Museum for providing information relating to several of the accounts. I am particularly grateful to Christine Bowman-Hill, Brian Dorey and Phil Murray for reading the manuscript and making helpful suggestions, and I stress that any errors or omissions are entirely my own.

# List of Contributors

Baden ALBIN, Bryony, Gill, Rachael and Raymond APLIN, Sue BARNES, Jamie BARTLETT, Gina and Nick BATHE, Claire BEALE, Paul and Sue BRENSON, Kate BROWN, Tracy BROWN, Cathy and Lea BOULTWOOD, John BURT, Emily CABLE, Dave CASWELL, Jasmine, Karen, Pippa, Tim and Trevor CATTLE, Rebecca CHARRON, Stacey CLARE-HOARE, Elly CLARKE, Judy CLEGG, Stephen COLEMAN, Janneane CONNOR, Ian COPPACK, David CORBEN, Geoff DENNIS, Selwyn DIMENT-DAVIES, Lukasz DOMAGALA, Brian DOREY, Melanie and Peter DYKE, Mary EASTMAN, Martin EGAN, Lucy and Mark ELFORD, Hugh ELMES, Jillian EMERY, Sandra ERSKINE, Peter FOOKS, Jacqui FORSTER, Angie HARRISON-PAGE, 'Harry', Norman HAYWARD, Rachel HELFER, Sacha HILDICH, Tina HILLS, Ben HOLDEN, Brian HORSEY, Lil HOSEGOOD, Lesley HOWLETT, Jsanine JENKIN, 'Kate', Linda KELLY, Mark KNIGHT, Joy LEATON, Tim LIGHTBOWNE, John LLOYD, Derek LOVELESS, Lara MANNINGHAM-BULLER, Helen MCCGWIRE, Jeremy MERCHANT, Mo and Phil MURRAY, Dwain MUSSELWHITE, 'Patricia', Kathryn PAYNE, Jacci PESTANA, Andy PETHICK, Jan POOLE, Terri POWELL, Andrew POWER, Andrew and Karen PURKIS, Eddie and Jan RAINFORD, Matthew RAWLINGS, Debbie REYNOLDS, Trevor RICH, Claire RICHARDS, Nicola RICHARDS, Amanda ROBINS, Charlotte and Richard ROSE, Lisa SAINSBURY, Reginald SAVILLE, Heather SEPHTON, Stuart SIMS, Pete SMITH, Roger SMITH, Jane SPENCER, Alf and Cherry STEARN, Amy STEELE, Laura SUTTLE, Marion TAYLOR, Jamie TRAFFORD, Laurice TURNER, Vickie WALTERS, Angela WATERMAN, Andrew WELCH, Brian WHITE, Krissy WHY, Brian WINTERS

# Introduction

## The Key-Hole View and Wider Vision

Imagine being imprisoned inside a castle tower, the only light to illuminate the darkness coming from an arrow slit in the wall. Then put your eye to the slit and gaze out on the narrow view that you are presented with; you cannot see far to the left or right and have even less idea of what may lie behind you, yet if you are incarcerated there for any lengthy period of time, you may begin to feel that this narrow view represents the whole of reality. Now imagine being released from the tower and standing on the top of the wall: the view has greatly widened and is all around you, so you can perceive it from different angles; the light is almost dazzling in intensity compared with the darkness inside the tower. Your perception of the world has increased considerably, which means that your consciousness has expanded: life has taken on a new dimension.

The view from the arrow slit is rather similar to how most of us perceive the world in our everyday lives: through a narrow perspective of what we call 'reality'. In purely physical terms, it is apparent that our senses are themselves very limited: our hearing, vision and smell are all within a certain range and can be poor in comparison with other life forms; neither can we harness electricity in the way that certain species of fish do, nor make use of vibrations as some animals and insects have become adept at. The outlook from the top of the wall represents a grand perspective, a kind of bird's-eye view, which some people may occasionally experience through mystical or heightened states of awareness, such as meditation or contemplation, and usually in brief glimpses or flashes. This 'grand' view may suggest that there is another reality other than the purely physical. Those who have had such experiences say how everything is interconnected, and it seems that these experiences may be linked to our intuitive mind, or 'right brain', as some scientists would say. The right brain is associated with art, music and poetry, while the left brain, the rational mind, is linked to language and logic. It is probable that man has developed the rational mind at the expense of the intuitive because modern societies are constructed in such a way that they demand rational thought in order to survive. Alongside this is the desire for clear, objective proof in a world of increasing uncertainty. Scientific discoveries have brought great benefits and, through misuse, some dangers to our world, and as scientists deal with physical phenomena, they demand objective proof. For some people, a fact can only be a fact if it can be verified empirically; in other words, through the use of our senses. Water, for instance, can be observed, and repeatedly observed, to boil at 100 degrees Celsius under normal conditions. The rational mind is being used here, just as it is in the case of solving a complex mathematical equation through deductive reasoning.

Experiences, however, are not always as straightforward as the rational mind leads us to believe, and our narrow, limited view is often perceived as the total reality rather than a partial answer. Light is essential to most forms of life as we understand it and we observe light all the time, yet the strange thing about it is that a photon (a quantum of light) can be both a wave and a particle. If a beam of light of a single colour is shone through a pair of narrow slits on a screen, the light waves emerging from the two holes reinforce each other to produce a characteristic pattern of bright and dark shapes on a second screen beyond, demonstrating the wave nature of light. If the light source is then made very faint, individual photons (particles) will pass through the slits one by one. It might be expected that the pattern of stripes would disappear if each photon has passed through either one slit or the other, but the same pattern of bright and dark shapes builds up with the arriving photons, which means that in some sense each individual photon passes through both slits. Don't worry if you don't really understand this as no physicist can explain it rationally! I only use this example to show that it is possible to observe a physical phenomenon that makes no sense to the rational mind.

Knowledge of something does not always depend on the rational mind. Some autistic savants have the ability to calculate almost instantaneously the answer to a difficult mathematical problem, working even faster than a computer could. In this case the knowledge is not obtained through deductive reasoning but through a kind of quantum leap, perhaps through intuition. How is it possible to know whether a painting, musical composition or poem is truly a great work of art? A more subjective element appears to have crept in here, yet instinctively many of us just seem to *know*, perhaps intuitively, that something is great, even though we cannot rationalise it very easily by putting it into words. Intuitive knowledge seems to be a case of perceiving something directly, rather than knowing something *about* it. How many of us have had the experience of walking along the street and suddenly receiving in our minds the image of a friend we have not seen for a long time, only to meet that person around the next corner? What kind of knowledge is this? And what about the numerous examples of premonitions of impending disaster, some of which led people to take evasive actions? Isn't this knowledge from a source other than the rational mind? What about those people who have either dreamed of or seen an apparition of a loved one at the moment of death or a crisis? Then there are others who have had the experience of looking down at themselves and their apparently lifeless bodies during some trauma and can recall the conversation of people around them. Knowledge, it would seem, comes in various forms, and we become aware of it in different ways.

It is my contention that much of what is termed 'paranormal' is perceived through the intuitive mind, which therefore makes it hard, if not impossible, to measure or record in a scientific laboratory. Some experiments in telepathy, precognition and psychokinesis (mind over matter), such as those carried out by J.B. Rhine at Duke University in the 1930s, have had a certain amount of success, but the most substantial evidence for the paranormal comes from people's personal experiences.

So what exactly *is* the 'paranormal' and how may it be defined? The paranormal is a term used to cover a range of phenomena, such as ghosts, poltergeist activity, out of the body and near death experiences, precognition, telepathy, psychokinesis, synchronicities and possibly UFO sightings. It could be defined as 'that which lies beyond the known laws of science and an understanding of which could lead to a significant shift in our way of perceiving the world and what may lie beyond'. A greater understanding could help to shed light on some of the most unfathomable mysteries that have puzzled mankind for millennia, the greatest of all being what happens to us when we die.

Many scientists are reluctant to trust 'evidence' that appears to be mainly subjective or anecdotal, yet when that evidence becomes accumulative and then overwhelming and contains thousands of accounts of paranormal experiences (the Society for Psychical Research, for instance, has been collecting accounts since the 19th century), many of which have common elements where a pattern begins to emerge, surely it is time to sit up and take note? Personal testimony in a court of law is also subjective, yet is regarded as admissible evidence. Science itself is undergoing a revolution in which theoretical physics is becoming almost as esoteric as anything paranormal. The idea of multiple parallel worlds, once the domain of science fiction, is now considered almost mainstream physics. The strange world of quantum mechanics, where the uncertainty principle states that an electron can be in different places simultaneously until a measurement is taken, is hard to get one's head around, while string theory opens up the possibility of extra spatial dimensions. Distinctions between subjectivity and objectivity are increasingly blurred and there are those who would even argue that an object only exists when we observe it (the arrogance of humans!). Reality is in a very real sense how we perceive things: we think of physical objects as being solid, yet at an atomic level they are masses of swirling particles, each atom containing a million billion times more empty space than solid matter. Our bodies, therefore, are full of empty space! Physicists are of the opinion that visible matter in the universe is only 4% of what is actually out there, with the rest consisting of 'dark matter' (invisible, but measurable and surrounding galaxies) and the even more mysterious 'dark energy' which is causing the universe to expand at an increasing rate. There is also the search for a 'Grand Unifying Theory' which would connect the quantum world with that of Einstein's world of relativity and space-time, in other words, the very small measurements used by quantum physics at the atomic level combined with the grand scale of the vast distances in the universe in one 'perfect' theory. The problem is that whenever we think we have reached the limit of human knowledge, it becomes apparent that we have only just started on the journey.

The above shows that, despite great advances in physics, there is still much that is not understood about the physical world and universe, let alone anything that may lie beyond it. This also applies to the workings of the human brain and whether the physical organ is separate from consciousness, as discussed in Chapter 4. Evolutionary biology very clearly explains how physical life forms have undergone transformations through natural selection and adaptation to environmental changes, but how consciousness came into being and why it should have done so is difficult to answer in purely biological terms, perhaps because it may not actually *be* physical. There is also the question of whether humans are the only species on the planet to have consciousness; in a sense, all species have an awareness of their environment as well as themselves and have evolved clever survival strategies over time in order to perpetuate their kind. Higher species of apes and also dolphins and whales seem to have a developed sense of self-awareness and show a high degree of intelligence when communicating with one another. The study of modern genetics has proved that all life forms are interconnected and illustrates how species evolved from common ancestors, so perhaps there was always a kind of in-built primeval consciousness, at least in a dormant state. It is therefore of great interest that one of the central features of mystical experiences, which transcend all narrow religious divisions, is the feeling of interrelatedness: man is not meant to have dominion over other species, but to be part of a greater whole. It is also noteworthy that other species, apart from man, appear to be aware of the paranormal: dogs in particular seem to be good at detecting 'ghosts', as will be seen in Chapters 1–3.

# Family Experiences and the Birth of the Book Paranormal Purbeck

As a boy I was fascinated by the paranormal because I began to realise that behind our everyday reality lies another world where apparently strange, or even 'impossible', things can happen. It all started with my own family. My father had an experience in which he found that he was looking down on his own body when he was not even ill at the time, clearly some kind of 'out-of-the body' experience. His background of being brought up in a narrow Christian evangelical environment coupled with his military service in the First World War had knocked the stuffing out of religion for him and he had no particular belief system, yet regarding death he once said that he thought it would be like walking into another room.

My maternal grandmother had the psychic ability to see ghosts/spirits, including that of her own husband who appeared to her by the garden gate about six weeks after he had died. During the Second World War my mother's brother Charles was serving in the army in the North African desert and my mother recalled that one day she found her own mother looking as white as a sheet. She told her that she had just had a vision of Charles and said, 'I think something terrible has happened to your brother'. A few weeks later, they received a telegram with the news that he had been severely wounded and had been given the last rites by a priest. Fortunately, he did not die, but went on to make a full recovery. It seemed that my grandmother's vision had occurred at the time of the near-fatal injury and that an apparition of Charles had been created telepathically. Many years later, I remember my mother having a dream about death, in which a figure in black appeared, the night before her 67th birthday. She thought it was meant for her, but she was wrong. The day after her birthday my Uncle Charles dropped dead in the street. This was a very clear example of a premonition.

My mother had several other paranormal experiences. As a young woman she had a dream about a serious accident in the street. The dream was broken when her own mother rushed into the bedroom to tell her that there had, indeed, just been a terrible accident outside. On another occasion she was taken to King's Lynn for the first time and amazed her family by describing correctly the different places they were about to see. Could she have had a precognitive dream about her forthcoming visit, I wonder, the subconscious memory of which was jogged on arrival in the town? I also recall an occasion when I visited the 16th century Byngley House in Poole with her and, on coming out, she said that she never wanted to go back there again. She had felt that something unpleasant had occurred in one of the upstairs bedrooms. At the time I was rather dismissive, but a year or so later I read an article in a local magazine that stated that a number of people had had similar experiences to my mother. The feeling was one of faintness and suffocation and it is interesting that the remains of a mummified cat were found nailed to some floor joists, which may have been done to counteract an evil spirit.

As for myself, I had a possible UFO sighting at the age of 13 when out walking with a friend near Swanage and, significantly, several other people saw strange lights in the sky an evening or so later. On occasions, time seems to jump ahead of itself for me, which has led me to conclude that our concept of linear time is wrong. There are also two experiences I will relate in connection with death. On the morning of my mother's funeral, I called in at the funeral directors to pay my final respects. As some readers may know, there is sometimes a distinctive, sickly sweet smell in a funeral parlour and that morning was no exception. When I returned home, I went into the lounge and suddenly noticed the same smell close to the chair where she used to sit so often. I mentioned this experience to only a few people, including a lady who had been an old friend of my mother's. Some years later, I attended her own funeral at Bournemouth crematorium; the short service being over, we had gone outside and the smoke had started to rise up, which we tried not to notice. Suddenly, perhaps due to a change in the wind direction, some of the smoke descended and hit me in the face and also several people near me. I did not think much more about it and later returned home. On opening the door and walking in, the first thing that immediately struck me was the smell of smoke. It was there for a brief moment and I was inclined to dismiss it as imagination, but on thinking it over later in the day, I came to the conclusion that with the lady's unusual sense of humour and her knowledge of what had happened on the day of my mother's funeral, it was exactly the kind of message she would have left, so typically her!

Most of the accounts in this book are based on personal interviews I conducted, and they have therefore never been published before; many were the result of calling at promising locations, but I also appealed on several occasions in the local press for people to come forward with paranormal stories. 'Paranormal Purbeck' was conceived in the spring of 2011. It has always seemed to be the most appropriate title: a book about the paranormal experiences of people living in (or, in a few cases, visiting) the Isle of Purbeck. I have included experiences from those living in Wareham as it is the gateway to Purbeck and contains a number of haunted locations. Occasionally, a few examples from outside Purbeck have also been given in order to illustrate a particular point.

The bulk of the material I have collected relates to haunted locations, apparitions and poltergeist activity and forms the basis for Chapters 1 and 2, with nearly 70 sites being described. I have tried to give clear details of these locations, though where a private address is involved, the name of the road is often just given and I should like to emphasise that no one reading this book should attempt to call on someone's family home. There were also several sites where it was not possible to give a precise location due to the need to protect certain individuals. Those unfamiliar with Purbeck may find local street maps of help. In Chapter 3 there is a detailed account of one remarkably haunted location, the Royal Oak in Swanage, with multiple phenomena being reported by nearly 40 eyewitnesses. Chapter 4 is a study of the phenomenon known as 'near death experiences' and the possibility that consciousness may be separate from the brain, with the evidence for survival beyond physical death being examined. The focus in Chapter 5 is on time, with accounts of precognitive dreams, premonitions and synchronicities (meaningful coincidences); our everyday understanding of time is also challenged. The subject of Chapter 6 is UFO sightings, including some local accounts. The final chapter considers the significance of the phenomena and tentatively draws a few conclusions.

It will be clear from the above that this book is more than just a collection of interesting and unusual personal experiences. What I have set out to show, by concentrating on a small geographical area, is that paranormal phenomena are widespread and may be experienced by many people who are open-minded, or at least intuitively receptive at a particular moment. Over 100 local people have contributed to the book and I am sure that this is just the tip of the iceberg. It would be possible, I believe, to take almost any location of similar extent, repeat the research and obtain comparable results. Throughout the book I attempt some analysis and offer a few explanations, though much will be reserved for the final chapter.

The case for paranormal phenomena is overwhelming for anyone prepared to examine the subject with an open mind, and this book offers a challenge in the form of personal evidence to all those who reject paranormal claims, whether they happen to be scientific reductionists, materialists or those of a particular religious persuasion. All these people have one thing in common: the keyhole vision, a limited view of the world based on preconceived ideas or beliefs and reinforced through the rational (sometimes 'irrational') mind. While it is both natural and desirable to raise doubts when unsubstantiated claims are made, there are some sceptics who are lazy and refuse to examine evidence properly. There are also those who do not like discussing the paranormal because they feel that in some way it goes against their belief system, or that it is dangerous. While there *are* aspects that can be harmful (for example, dabbling in Black Magic, using the ouija board, some possible cases of possession and certain poltergeist manifestations), the vast majority of the phenomena described in this book are not and there is much that we can learn from studying the paranormal about our own subconscious and worlds that may lie beyond. Most of the fear associated with the paranormal is fear of the unknown. Those who mistakenly refer to it all in negative terms because of their religious beliefs should consider the millions who have died, or suffered, as a result of the bigotry and intolerance that have characterised so many religions throughout history. 'Paranormal Purbeck', in fact, is all about people's experiences, not about beliefs. What came across particularly when I was interviewing people about their paranormal experiences was that the vast majority had no preconceptions, which I found very refreshing. What also struck me was how genuine these experiences seemed to be and I certainly never got the impression that anyone was trying to deceive me.

# Chapter 1

# Paranormal Activity in the Studland, Swanage and Langton Matravers Areas

This chapter contains accounts of ghostly phenomena and other paranormal activity from south-east Purbeck, covering Studland, Swanage, Langton Matravers and Harmans Cross. In most cases the stories refer to specific locations, though a few are more concerned with individuals. The majority of apparitions described fall under the 'haunting' category, where they are experienced in a particular location over a period of time. Contrary to popular belief, most 'ghosts' or 'spirits' (disembodied entities) do not generally occur in graveyards. Some of the haunted locations in this chapter (and also Chapters 2 and 3) appear to have poltergeist activity accompanying sightings of ghosts. The traditional explanation for a poltergeist is that it is a mischievous, or sometimes malevolent, spirit that typically causes loud noises, objects to move and sometimes bad smells, but others would argue that it is a living person subconsciously projecting a psychokinetic (mind over matter) force, perhaps as a result of emotional disturbance. It is probable that both explanations may apply according to the case that is being considered.

## Studland

### Manor House Hotel

The Manor House Hotel, Manor Road, Studland, has almost unrivalled views across its extensive grounds towards Studland Bay and beyond to the coastline of Bournemouth. The main building dates from around 1825, but incorporates an earlier one, and was erected as a seaside residence for George Henry Bankes and his family, who owned much land in the area, including Corfe Castle. Following the death of Ralph Bankes in 1981, the estate passed to the National Trust. The house itself became a hotel soon after the Second World War.

Paranormal activity has been reported here on a few occasions. Richard

Rose was the proprietor for 35 years up until 2000 and his parents ran it before him. He described how on one occasion he had been serving drinks behind the bar when, out of the corner of his eye, he saw a tall figure wearing a cape enter the small room to the left adjacent to the bar. When he went across to look into the room, the figure had vanished. Richard saw the figure on several subsequent occasions, but said nothing about it to his wife, Charlotte. Sometime afterwards (Charlotte thought it was about 1987), she had a very similar experience: she was standing in the bar around 11 p.m. with her back to the menu board and having a conversation when she saw a man enter the same small room to the left. Curious about what she had witnessed, she went into the room and discovered that the man had apparently disappeared into the wall! Charlotte described him as being in his 30s, very tall and wearing a black cape; his hair was done up in a bunch. When she mentioned it to Richard, he said, 'You've seen the ghost as well!' The area where the sightings occurred is the oldest part of the building and may date to around 1750. Charlotte also told me that a woman she knew had reported seeing a man in a cape when she had been driving through Studland, though whether this was the same figure is not clear. After Charlotte's experience, neither of them saw the figure again. It is possible that the figure may be the same as that experienced by Karen Purkis at Manor Farmhouse, described below.

Andrew Purkis was the proprietor of the Manor House Hotel from 2000 until 2012 and he told me that one persistent ghost story relates to the 'Blue Lady', who may have been seen by a number of people. She is described as having a long flowing dress and seems to have been seen mostly in the bar entrance. Kate Brown used to help her mother when she was working in

*Manor House Hotel, Studland*

the hotel in about 1990 and said they were aware of the story of the Blue Lady, who would apparently call out for her child around the stairway. Kate heard the voice on one occasion and her mother experienced it a number of times. Phil Murray recalled being told in the early 1970s about the Blue Lady, who was reported to have been seen at Studland, particularly in association with the Manor House Hotel. It was said that she was terrifying to look at, but if you had enough courage to follow her, you would find buried treasure! Richard and Charlotte Rose believe that this story may have its origins in a fictional work entitled *Strange Adventures in the County of Dorset*, a smuggling tale set at the Manor House. One of the bedrooms in the story has a portrait of a lady in a blue dress, who is supposed to haunt the room; she was said to be the daughter of a previous owner, became pregnant and was sent abroad in disgrace, where she died giving birth to the child. The interesting question here is whether the author based this on a real ghost story, or if some genuine paranormal experiences have been mistakenly connected to a fictitious story.

Andrew Purkis mentioned a few other possible paranormal incidents that have occurred at the hotel. In the downstairs bedroom suite, an elderly couple reported a cup of tea falling onto the floor of its own volition. This happened twice in succession, with both of them witnessing the cup falling off the window ledge the second time. The Coach House, which dates from the early 18th century, used to be the staff quarters. One young man felt his bedclothes being pulled off him in the night and the mother (a medium) of another member of staff said that she could not go into the room. The building has now been converted into guest bedrooms. Several couples have reported waking up in the night and feeling unusually cold when the weather has not been so.

The Manor House Hotel closed for refurbishment in 2013 and is under new management.

## Manor Farmhouse

Andrew Purkis, former proprietor of the Manor House Hotel, lived at Manor Farmhouse, close to St Nicholas's Church, with his wife Karen from 2000 until 2013. The building, which is now divided into two sections as the result of a dispute that occurred between the previous owners, consists of one part dating from the late 17th century and a newer part from the 1820s, which is where Andrew and his family lived. Andrew said that he thought there had been a lot of unhappiness associated with the property and that the previous owners may have had children who had died there.

Andrew described a number of paranormal experiences that had occurred at Manor Farmhouse. The most dramatic concerned his wife Karen, who had woken up one night to find a man dressed in black, in appearance like a highwayman, standing by the bed with his hands outstretched. She thought he was going to strangle her, but instead he stroked her hair. Some while later, their stepson, who had not been told of the appearance of this strange figure, reported seeing a similar man in black standing at the top of the stairs leading down to the cellar.

Andrew also related how a few years previously the wicker chair in his baby daughter's bedroom would sometimes creak as though someone was sitting in it when there was no one there. On a different occasion there appeared to be some resistance to the door being opened. Another strange incident occurred one Christmas morning when some tinsel, which had been draped over a clock in the kitchen, started shaking. Andrew went over to examine this but could find no logical explanation. Karen told me that a number of photographs taken in the house a few years ago showed orbs (small circles which some claim are signs of paranormal activity).

Their daughter Portia had an imaginary friend called Lucy when she was under 2 years old. This 'imaginary friend' was so persistent that Karen once asked Portia if her friend Lucy would like a drink and she replied that she would like some ale, which seemed quite strange for a young child to say. Lucy became such a feature that Andrew and Karen even visited the churchyard to see if they could find the name on any of the gravestones, but were unsuccessful.

## Bankes Arms

Derek Loveless has lived in Studland all his life and works as a ranger supervisor for the National Trust. He has a vivid recollection of a paranormal experience that occurred to him in the Bankes Arms around 1974/5. Derek told me that he would occasionally stay in the pub to look after it when the landlord was away, and one memorable winter night he was sleeping in Room 1. He described how he woke up from a deep sleep in the middle of the night to see the apparition of a woman filling the doorway. She was tall and dressed in a 'Maid Marian' type outfit, which included a veil and a hat. Derek said he did not feel frightened, but was transfixed by the apparition and could not look away. After the figure had vanished, he went back to sleep. The next day he told the landlord about his experience, but he was unable to shed any light on it.

Tim Lightbowne has been the landlord of this popular pub since the early 1980s. He said that several times a year he has felt the presence of

*Bankes Arms, Studland*

a man in a grey frock coat in the Horseshoe Bar. The man appears by the door at the west side of that room, walks across and disappears through the wall where a door used to be many years ago. Tim said that the presence always occurs in winter during bad weather.

Barmaid Sacha Hildich described how in the autumn of 2011 an empty half-pint glass had been placed on top of another on the bar counter. Suddenly and for no apparent reason the top glass had exploded, with the bottom one remaining undamaged. Sacha found this very puzzling as neither glass had been hot at the time. In October 2012 Sacha related a similar incident that had occurred earlier that month when an empty pint glass had been placed over another upside down on the shelf below the bar; the bottom part of the top glass had then exploded despite the fact that the glasses were cold and had been standing there for several hours.

## The White Donkey

In the 1969 winter edition of *Dorset, the County Magazine*, Benjamin Pond related an experience he had had on Studland Heath on the night of 22 December 1929, which he described as the most frightening of his life. He worked as a fisherman and would sometimes leave his boat at Shell Bay and walk back across the heath to his shack at Goathorn, a distance of 4 miles.

On the night in question he had moored his boat in Shell Bay at around 11.30 p.m. and set out on his lonely walk over the heath. It was after about a mile and a half that he suddenly saw a mysterious white object on the track ahead and fear began to grip him. On realising it was only a white donkey, he felt relief, but his fears soon returned when the object suddenly

*Studland Heath*

vanished. The next morning Benjamin returned to the spot, but could find no hoof marks and on making enquiries discovered that no white donkeys were roaming the area. Several months later he learned that other men had seen the apparition of the donkey, which seemed to appear on the same date he had experienced it. It transpired that about 160 years previously, a man had been riding a white donkey near Bramble Bush Bay three nights before Christmas when he was attacked and murdered by a navy deserter. The murdered man's money and rum were stolen; the donkey ran away.

Rebecca Charron, who lives at Knitson, believes she may also have seen the ghost of the donkey. She remembers as a young girl (probably in the late 1960s) travelling by car along the Ferry Road when it was dark, possibly returning from a Christmas show in Bournemouth. They had passed the toll booth (in those days situated south-east of the sewage works) and were approaching the turning to Knoll car park, when Becca suddenly saw a white donkey walking on the verge on the opposite side of the road. She recalls being worried that the donkey might get knocked down by a car. Later, she was told it was a ghost and that the donkey had been seen there before.

There are several particularly interesting aspects to this ghost story. First, it is rare to hear about any ghost animals in Purbeck and ghost donkeys must surely be unusual generally, though I have recently come across two stories in Surrey. Second, it is curious that the haunting is not of the murdered man but of the animal he was riding. Finally, how would a ghost 'know' the 'correct date' to appear?

# Swanage

## A fishy smell in north Swanage

A Swanage resident described an experience that she, her husband and son had all had at a house they owned in the north of Swanage. The experience occurred in the early 1980s when the property was being let and a cleaner would come in from time to time to do some work.

The lady said that on a number of occasions they experienced a strong, unpleasant smell, like stale fish, in different parts of the property and felt that it emanated from some kind of entity or negative energy. They tried to remove it through prayer and eventually it did, in fact, go. The lady attributes it to the cleaner's daughter, who suffered from a mental illness and had come into the house with her mother on one or two occasions. When the girl returned to hospital, there were no more manifestations, so perhaps she had triggered the phenomenon.

It does seem that mental disturbance can either create or attract psychic phenomena.

## A mother's last intervention?

When Cherry Stearn left Swanage at 5.30 a.m. she knew her mother was seriously ill at Kettering Hospital in Northamptonshire and was determined to get there before she died. Her mother, however, was equally determined that she did not want her daughter to see her dying.

Cherry had been driving for about one and a half hours and was on the M27 when suddenly everything cut out, just as if the ignition had been switched off. Fortunately she managed to freewheel the car to a coned area and called the RAC. A man arrived after about 15 minutes and towed the car to the nearest garage. It transpired that one of the wires had come out of the fan belt and the problem was soon fixed. The delay had cost Cherry one hour and she then resumed her journey.

As soon as Cherry arrived at Kettering Hospital, she was told she was too late: her mother had died one hour before. When she saw her mother, there were no wrinkles on her face and her hair appeared to have a pink tinge. Cherry realised that had she not been delayed, she would have got there just in time, but her mother had said she did not want her to see her. Was there some way in which her mother had intervened in the last moments of her earthly life?

# The strange story of 'Miss Shiner'

Jacqui Forster works as a researcher and helper at Swanage Museum. In 2008 her then next-door neighbour in Swanage told her that her 7-year-old daughter had a 'friend' whom she called 'Miss Shiner'. The young girl told her mother that Miss Shiner had been with them at their previous address in Kings Road, Swanage, and on the day they moved house to the Bell Street area, she had got into the car with them. According to her, Miss Shiner was a pretty young lady who stayed in her bedroom in the new house and would stand at the end of her bed. The girl's mother was quite concerned by what her daughter had said and was particularly struck by the use of the surname 'Miss Shiner', which was unusual.

Soon after Jacqui had been told this, she happened to be doing some research into burial records for someone else. Imagine her surprise when she came across the name 'Shiner' and then discovered that a young lady of that name had died tragically in Swanage. After doing some research, Jacqui found that a very detailed description of the young woman's funeral had appeared in the *Swanage Times* of 27 November 1926.

Kathleen May Shiner was born in 1904 and was the only child of Tom and Emma Kate Shiner, who ran a bathing tent business based in Shore Road, Swanage. The business had been carried on from Tom's father, Thomas, who claimed to have introduced mixed bathing to Swanage in 1879. The Shiners lived at Ivy Cottage, Shore Road. In October 1926 Kathleen, who was a milliner by profession, went to stay at Charlton Musgrove near Wincanton for a 5-week holiday, returning home on Wednesday 17 November. According to the *Swanage Times*, she was in good health on her return, apart from a small swelling on her forehead. On the Thursday night a doctor was called for advice and he said that an operation was necessary. This was carried out, but Kathleen died in the early hours on Friday morning, with the cause of death being given as acute meningitis. Her death certificate, a copy of which I obtained, states that the causes of death were cellulitis of the forehead (she had suffered from this for 5 days) and septic meningitis; no post mortem was carried out.

Kathleen's funeral took place three days after her death and it is clear from the 75 floral tributes that it would have been a highly emotional occasion; this comes across in words such as 'harp with broken strings', 'Earth hath one gentle soul less, and heaven one angel more' and 'Sweetest thoughts shall ever linger, round the grave where thou art laid'. Kathleen is described in the *Swanage Times* as being 'held in very high esteem by all with whom she came in contact', and that 'profound regret is expressed throughout the neighbourhood at the extremely sad loss'. Her grave can be seen on the west side of Northbrook Cemetery, situated near the railway bridge a few minutes' walk from Swanage town centre. The emotion that her death evoked is reinforced by the words on the stone: 'The charmed circle broken, a dear face missed day by day from its accustomed place'.

By the time Jacqui Forster gave the information on Kathleen Shiner to her next-door neighbour, the appearances of 'Miss Shiner' to the young girl had ceased; the sightings had lasted for a period of about 6 months. Unfortunately, the mother and daughter later moved from Swanage, so it was not possible for me to interview them. Was the 'Miss Shiner' seen by the little girl that of Kathleen? If so, why that particular child and why after more than 80 years after Kathleen's death? Children do have imaginary friends, but 'Miss Shiner' was persistent and it is an unusual name. Kathleen's untimely death certainly aroused considerable grief and it seems emotion is a key factor in creating paranormal phenomena.

## Gannets Park: the return of C.S. Lewis

The well-known theologian and biblical scholar Canon J.B. Phillips lived in Gannets Park, Swanage, with his wife Vera for many years. According to Phillips, the spirit of C.S. Lewis, the author of the Narnia chronicles and other books, appeared to him soon after Lewis's death in 1963 in order to offer advice. Lewis was also a Christian and had corresponded with Phillips on the subject of life after death, but they had only met once. Phillips described the apparition as radiant and grinning broadly at his host's unease. The figure made a second appearance the following week at the same time, once again to offer helpful advice. When Phillips asked how he was able to remain alive, Lewis is supposed to have replied, 'My dear fellow, this sort of thing is happening all the time!'

This seems to be a classic case of a post-mortem apparition, or disembodied spirit.

## A haunted premises

The exact location of this site in the Swanage area cannot be revealed, but it is a substantial building and paranormal phenomena have been experienced there for at least 30 years; an exorcism, or cleansing, also took place. The activity, as at so many other sites, was intermittent and seemed to increase when building work was being carried out, with a number of people experiencing it. One ghost that appears (and there was a sighting as recently as 2011) is that of a young girl, believed to be that of a person who was killed in a riding accident on a nearby farm. Other phenomena relate to a German pilot from the Second World War, who is thought to have crash-landed in the area and was then taken to the building, where he died. There have also been several reports of electrical equipment being interfered with.

One cleaner, referred to here by the pseudonym 'Harry', worked in the building for 10 years and had not been aware that any paranormal activity had been recorded there before his first experience. He had started work early in the morning and on entering one particular room had the unpleasant sensation of feeling cold, with his hair standing up. Harry then propped open all the doors to do the cleaning more quickly, but suddenly a loud bang occurred and all the doors closed. 'Anybody around?' he called out. As he started to vacuum, he could hear a loud noise like the sound of an aircraft above the noise of the cleaner. When he moved to another room, he heard what appeared to be the sound of an aircraft descending and the terrible screaming of a man in agony. Harry left the rooms three times to tell other people about what he was experiencing and eventually two other cleaners returned with him, with all three of them then hearing the noise. Harry also had a similar experience in the same location about 5–6 years later. Presumably, the noise of the aircraft and screaming refers to the German pilot, whose aircraft crash-landed in the area.

Some other people have also had uncomfortable experiences in that part of the building, such as feeling cold, the sensation of being watched and the impression that someone was going past. Two young men reported hearing the sound of screaming as if someone were in trouble. Harry recalled that a former cleaner had remarked that he had seen a young girl wearing old-fashioned white clothes, who had mysteriously disappeared in the same part of the building.

## The Parade

Linda Kelly lives with her partner Lea in a flat on the Parade. Their bedroom is situated in the basement and Linda described how on the first night they moved in during November 2011 she heard footsteps above the bedroom, which would have been coming from the lounge. A lady who had lived there previously reported that she had experienced the same phenomenon. On another night Linda said that she was in the bedroom with the door ajar and heard the sound of what seemed like something being thrown on three separate occasions, the noise apparently coming from within the room.

Linda has seen the figure of a man in white standing in the lounge and subsequently experienced this figure in dreams. Lea said that the dogs sometimes behaved strangely when they were in the lounge: they would sit and look towards the large cabinet as if someone were talking to them;

when they were outside, they would stare at one particular corner. When I revisited them in October 2012, both Linda and Lea confirmed that the dogs had stopped behaving unusually; Linda attributes this to her closing what she described as a 'portal' and the use of crystals.

## The Ship Inn

The Ship Inn is one of a number of pubs in the lower High Street, which is at the heart of the town. Over the years it has undergone extensive refurbishment.

Claire Beale works as a cleaner at the Ship and spoke to me in late November 2011, describing first an experience she had had one morning almost a year before: on that occasion she was vacuuming by the cupboard entrance near to the men's toilet and noticed a black figure caught on the CCTV monitor which is situated in the cupboard; the figure was outside the gents and had been picked up on the camera facing it. Claire immediately looked over to the gents but could see nothing, and then glanced back to the screen, but the figure had vanished.

A second experience occurred in the early summer of 2011 when she was sitting with her mother at the bar drinking tea around 12 p.m. after the pub had closed. They heard footsteps behind them and, on turning, saw

*Ship Inn, Swanage*

a black shadow running towards the corridor leading to the men's toilet. Claire told me that she feels uneasy in the building and often sees shadows out of the corner of her eye.

## Comforting experiences

Phil Murray, long-term resident of Swanage, had several unusual experiences while in the coronary unit at Poole Hospital during January/February 2012. After having anaesthetic for a transoesophageal echo (TOE) scan on 24 January, he had a dream about a very green, leafy grotto, where there were other people. Phil said that he knew there was danger for the other people (but not himself) and he had to guide them through; he had the sensation of floating/surfing with them. There was no sense of smell in his dream, but it was light and soft and the experience was pleasant. Phil had had ten previous TOE scans under identical conditions with the same local anaesthetic and was usually aware of most of the proceedings; nothing like this had occurred before.

Phil told me that every night after midnight (and also frequently during the day) he had the sensation that someone had sat down on the corner of his bed, as he could feel a definite weight and the bed sagging a little. He also got the feeling that someone wanted to put a hand on his thigh, with the experience being pleasant, not frightening. Despite sometimes sleeping without a sheet over him (as it was hot in the hospital), he had felt what appeared to be a sheet being pushed down. He was also aware of the displacement of air as if people had gone past. The awareness of movement towards and away from him and the pressure on the bed was in more than one place, the strongest being on his right side, as if someone had sat there.

*Phil Murray*

While Phil was on some medication, it should be noted that he was not taking hallucinatory drugs; the medication was the same he had been taking for the past 10 years for blood pressure and the antibiotics the same as the previous years, so there was nothing new, and his temperature readings were normal. On a previous occasion in hospital, he had had unpleasant hallucinations after being given certain drugs; he described the experiences this time as being very different and certainly positive. It was almost as though someone, or something, was trying to comfort him in preparation for what lay ahead: he subsequently had two major operations in March 2012, followed by complications where his life was in the balance. Fortunately, he made a full recovery.

Phil is a close friend of mine and during the 2-month period when he was at Southampton Hospital with his wife Mo at his bedside, I would go into their flat to feed their two ginger cats. Phil's life was in danger throughout this period, but there was one week in particular when his condition was especially grave. During that critical week both cats (and one is fairly young and normally very active) changed their behaviour and were noticeably lethargic and spent most of the time sleeping. There was nothing very different about the weather to account for it and it seemed almost as if they were in sympathy with Phil. Mo has a close bond with these cats and that week was one of the most stressful of her life. Could they in some way have tuned into her feelings from a distance?

## Manor Road

Claire Beale and her family have experienced paranormal activity in their house in Manor Road, where they have lived for a few years. According to Claire, many of the incidents that have occurred seem childish, such as lights going on and off, and child-like footsteps have been heard. The activity started soon after they moved in. Claire's mother witnessed one amazing incident when she saw a loaf of bread fly from the pantry shelf into the kitchen – a distance of about 12 ft! The eldest daughter had the experience of being pulled off the bed by her leg early one evening and Claire had the quilt pulled off her bed on one occasion in the night. Another time there was an exaggerated wave effect with Claire's bedroom curtains and the television itself on after 1 a.m. One of the most dramatic incidents occurred in her brother's room when he was with four friends: a blank CD from an open drawer shot up into the air and shattered.

## The Red Lion

The Red Lion situated in the High Street, Swanage, has been a well-patronised pub for many years. Karen Cattle, who has run the pub since about 2003, believes that the building may date back to the 17th century and was originally three cottages.

Karen said she had lived in haunted houses before and was therefore immediately aware on moving into the Red Lion that there was paranormal activity going on; her husband, daughter and mother-in-law also felt that the pub was haunted. Karen's other daughter, Pippa, had several strange experiences when she came with her husband to stay for Christmas 2006. Pippa recalled that it was late evening on Christmas Day and her husband had gone upstairs; she was down in the pool room area and saw what appeared to be the shadow of a man sitting in the window seat near the fireplace. On possibly the same night, she felt someone brush past her on the landing and felt the floorboards move.

According to Karen, three customers have said they believe that the pub has ghosts and she thinks that the man her daughter saw may have been the former landlord, 'Fred the Red', a well-known local character. Paranormal activity seems to occur after his wife has been in the pub. Apparently, objects, such as keys, have been moved and ashtrays found upside down (Fred had a reputation for playing practical jokes). Karen has had the strange experience, as have others, of hearing her name called near the cellar door. Karen's mother-in-law, Jasmine, said that there was also supposed to be the ghost of an old lady bewailing the fact that part of her kitchen had been turned into a bathroom. Karen's grandson, Tommy, apparently said (at the age of about three) that a little boy was crying in the corner of one of the bedrooms.

*Red Lion, Swanage*

Krissy Why, speaking in November 2011, said she had worked at the Red Lion for 4 years and had lived in the pub for three. She described how her partner had woken up in the night about 2 years before with the feeling of a weight on his chest and had seen the shadow of a man bending over Krissy. She then went on to tell me about an almost identical experience that had occurred to her current partner only 7 months previously when they were in the attic bedroom; her partner said he thought it must have been a dream. Then there was the occasion when a picture with a fairy on it had fallen off a shelf in the flat upstairs for no apparent reason; soon afterwards, Krissy had gone into the bottle store where the video monitor is kept and suddenly found her partner's engagement ring, which had been lost for 8 months, on the floor. As with Karen, Krissy spoke of activity around the cellar door, including the feeling of arms being placed around her. A former employee even claimed her bottom had been pinched!

A barman described how one beer pump in the main bar seemed to move of its own accord as he would sometimes find it in the down position. The pump is actually quite stiff and should go back slowly, so it is difficult to see how it could move far of its own volition. Karen later confirmed that all the bar staff had seen the pump move and that an object had now been placed in position to stop it moving forward.

## Cumberland Flats

Kate Brown used to live in the Cumberland Flats, Ilminster Road, and regularly experienced paranormal activity in the evenings there. She described how the television would turn itself off at 9.30 p.m. after the news had finished and she would then feel something pass through the room and hear doors open as though the 'presence' had moved on. Kate said that the flats had once been a nursing home.

The Cumberland Flats were demolished during the summer of 2012.

## Purbeck House Hotel

Purbeck House Hotel, situated in the High Street, was originally built by George Burt (sometimes referred to as 'the King of Swanage') as a private residence. Later, it became a Roman Catholic school run by nuns before being turned into a hotel. Some paranormal activity has been reported on occasions. A visitor to the hotel related an experience that had taken place late one evening at the beginning of 2011. She was walking along the corridor downstairs after coming out of the ladies and caught sight of a woman's figure in the lounge as she was going past it. The woman was elderly and wearing a long black skirt and white blouse with a shawl over it. The visitor described feeling at the time quite shaky and she walked on as quickly as possible. She mentioned what she had seen to a member of staff, but on investigation there was no sign of the woman in the lounge.

## The Mill Pond

Cathy Boultwood used to clean for an elderly lady living in a cottage at the Mill Pond. The lady's mother had died in the cottage and Cathy said she would have conversations in her mind with the lady's spirit while she was working. A kettle was kept on the floor and one day, while Cathy was wiping the window sill, she saw that it had turned itself on. This happened on a few more occasions and Cathy eventually told the old lady, who was very interested.

Sometime later, Cathy was dusting a shelf in the old lady's bedroom and remarked to the lady, who was in bed at the time, that the kettle had turned itself on again. 'Who do you think it is?' Cathy asked. The lady replied that she thought it was her twin sister, who had died when she was 6 months old. She then asked Cathy who she thought it was and Cathy responded, 'I think it's your mother'. At that point Cathy felt what she described as a vortex of energy, like a whirlpool, from her feet to her head; it lasted seconds, but was very intense.

## Argyle Road: a poltergeist case

Elly Clarke described how a poltergeist, or spirit, had followed her from a property in Canford Heath to one in Argyle Road, Swanage. The house in Canford Heath was situated in a cul-de-sac and Elly thought the properties might have been built over an old burial site. There were disturbances in the house and structural damage that Elly attributed to the entity, and also the smell of stale fish and cigar smoke. In 1993 Elly and her husband had the opportunity to move permanently to Swanage and she 'invited' the entity to come with them because she felt that if she did not, the entity might prevent them from leaving the Canford Heath house by causing more structural damage, which would then require them to stay longer to carry out more repair work.

The house they moved to is a Victorian semi-detached property. She remembered how the little girl next door would talk to a man whom she said 'would come out of the chimney'. Elly described how electrical equipment was affected at their own property: lights would go on and off and the stereo would change channels. On one occasion the top of a bottle flicked off before she had time to use the bottle opener.

When she was pregnant with her first son, Elly remembered waking up and seeing a man's face right up close: she described it as serene and loving. After the birth of her first son, she recalled how the cot would move across the room upstairs, the sound of which she could hear below. On one memorable occasion she found the baby not only was out of his cot, but also had been moved from one end of the room to the other. The entity remained after her second son was born in 2005. In 2006 she took a photograph of orbs, in which her eldest son appeared to follow them with his fingers. Elly left the property in 2009 and the entity has not followed her to her present address.

## Argyle Road: the sailor's return?

I am grateful to a Swanage man for the following account, which would date to one summer in the mid-1950s. The property in question (not the same as the one in the above account) offered bed and breakfast during the holiday season and this story concerns a couple that visited who had never been to the town before, or had any connections with it.

Not long after the couple had started their holiday and breakfast was being served in the sitting room, the woman said to the landlady, 'A sailor used to live in this house, didn't he?' The landlady had known the road throughout her life: she had been born there before the First World War, her sister and two aunts had lived in it for a considerable number of years, and she herself had lived within 150 yards of it since birth and had moved there, eventually to be joined by her husband, shortly after the Second World War. It therefore came as a surprise to her that a visitor should know about a former occupant who had been dead for many years and it was inevitable therefore that she should ask, 'However do you know that?' The reply was short and to the point: 'I met him on the stairs last night'. Somewhat taken aback, the landlady left the room and the couple began their breakfast. The subject of the stranger on the stairs was not raised throughout the remainder of the couple's holiday and they never returned to the house again.

It is believed that the sailor lived in the house sometime between the two World Wars. There was an inexpensive tin wall plaque on the stairs of a 17th century galleon where the apparition was seen, so could this have formed some kind of psychic link?

# Court Hill

Angie Harrison-Page lives in a property in Court Hill, which dates to the early 20th century. Angie, a medium, has experienced a variety of phenomena at the property. Her father worked as an electronics engineer and died in about 2000; Angie told me she sometimes feels his presence, such as the stereo turning itself on, the smell of tobacco and the rocking chair moving. During the time of the loft conversion, the bedroom door would swing open and she had images of children, with one in particular being that of a little girl whom she thinks had been run over by a cart and taken to the house where she died. She also felt the presence there of a man, whom she has 'moved on' (so the 'spirit' is no longer attached to that particular place), as well as the people who had lived there prior to her.

Interestingly, the parish records show that an Elizabeth Bishop died in Swanage on 24 July 1840 at the age of one after being run over by the wheel of a wagon going over her head. The site of the accident is not given, but could it have been close to where Angie now lives?

# The face at Newton Manor School

Newton Manor was a girls' private school, which closed some years ago; the buildings have since been converted into private residences. The following story was recounted by Rachael Aplin, who was a pupil at the school, and the experience she described relates to about 1975 when she would have been 14.

Rachael and her friend Celeste had been given a detention in the art room, which was located in a different building from the main school. The art room was on the top floor of this building and separated from the science laboratory by a flight of stairs. Rachael and Celeste were sitting in the art room doing their detention with no one else present when Rachael noticed a face at eye level under the sink where the pipes were. She described the face as being that of a man with long black hair and a long black beard and having a Jacobean appearance. Rachael drew Celeste's attention to the face and both girls felt very unnerved by it as it remained there for some minutes. As they were both frightened by what they had seen, they went down to the science laboratory to finish their detention, where they were later reprimanded by a teacher for leaving the art room without permission.

A few years later, Rachael and Celeste were doing another detention, this time in the library. Rachael chose a book to copy out of and, on opening it, saw a face, which she recognised as the one they had previously seen in the art room. She showed the picture to Celeste, who agreed that the face was very similar. According to Rachael, the name given to the face in the book was 'Jaques', which is interesting as one of the previous owners of Newton Manor apparently had this name.

Rachael said that Newton Manor had a reputation for being haunted and that several of the cleaners refused to work in the science laboratory, where the potter's wheel would sometimes go round of its own volition. Another former pupil, Emily Cable, said that she had experienced an uncomfortable feeling in the classroom near the art room.

Newton Cottage, which was destroyed by a bomb in the Second World War, was situated on the south side of the road. A former owner of Newton Manor, Sir Charles Robinson, said that Newton Cottage was haunted. Nearby some of the body parts from five victims of Monmouth's rebellion, executed at Wareham in 1685, were displayed from a post supported by the gallows stone.

## The Grange, High Street

Selwyn Diment-Davies described a number of paranormal experiences in relation to his caring for an elderly lady in a building known as 'The Grange' (originally 'The Old Orchard') which had belonged to Newton Manor. In particular, he experienced very cold areas in the building (Selwyn said that he does not normally feel the cold) and what he termed an icy cold presence that would make his hair stand on end. According to him, there was a feeling of pure evil around the lady's room and the corridor, and this evil force was getting stronger as the old lady was dying. Selwyn said that he thought the problem had been in the land rather than the building itself. A Church of England vicar performed a ceremony upstairs in the presence of Selwyn and also another carer and Selwyn described how he felt as if a male entity had brushed past him. The house then became easier and the old lady died a month later.

## Visions of her father

Janneane Connor lives in Swanage and related a number of experiences she had had in connection with her father, who died on 17 January 2012. She said she had been very close to him.

On the evening following his death, Janneane went round to a friend's house, where church meetings are regularly held. A minute's prayer took place and Janneane closed her eyes: she could see a yellow object and then made out her father standing in what appeared to be a kind of queue. He was dressed in a leather jacket and trousers and had curly hair; he looked in his late forties, so appeared about 30 years younger than when he had died. Janneane was looking at him from a few yards away and her view was that of a side profile. She could also make out the shapes of other people behind and in front of him and it was clear that he could not move forward. At no time did he look at her.

On 6 February 2012, 3 days after the funeral, Janneane went to the cemetery to have a look at the grave which, she found to her amazement, had dropped by several feet in that very short time. One of the council workmen in the cemetery told her that he had never known a grave drop like that. Janneane responded by saying, 'You don't think he's got out, do you?' It was just after she had spoken those words that she heard her name 'Jans' called twice, the name that her father used for her.

On 1 May Janneane got up in the night at around 2 a.m. to go to the toilet. While she was there, with the door ajar, she saw her father walk from her daughter's bedroom into the living room. The figure appeared solid and was walking at a normal pace; she could see the back of his head (but not his face) and a stripey t-shirt. Janneane felt he had come to see the results of a Chelsea football match, which she said he would have taken great interest in during his life.

On another occasion Janneane had a dream in which a round yellow object came close to her face. She could make out a man's face with curly hair and two horns at the side of the head, but she could not be certain if the dream was related to her father. Janneane has felt her hand being touched and also her shoulder, which she does attribute to her father.

Janneane's aunt, Cathy Boultwood, described an experience that could also be related to the death of Janneane's father. Quite soon after he had died, she woke up one night to go to the toilet. After getting back into bed and lying down, she opened her eyes and saw a yellow orb in the corner of the room near the ceiling, which disappeared in seconds. There does seem to be an association with the colour yellow in connection with Janneane's father's death, but the significance of it remains a mystery.

## A young girl's visit

Peter Fooks, who has lived in Swanage all his life, described an experience he had in the early 1980s at a property in the High Street where he and his wife were living. He woke up one night to find a young girl standing by the bed and looking at him, which made him jump with surprise. The girl was standing immediately to his left and his wife was asleep by his side on his right. Peter said that the girl was pretty, aged around six or seven, and was wearing an old-fashioned white dress. He did not feel afraid and described the experience as pleasant. Could it be the case that the girl had lived and perhaps died at the property?

## Disturbances at a cottage

Cathy Boultwood lived in a cottage in the High Street for 2 years. She recalled drifting off to sleep one night and then being aware of a flash, such as would come from a flash bulb, when her eyes were closed; this happened on several occasions. (Subsequently, a tenant reported the same experience.) She also described how she would be in the bath downstairs and would distinctly hear the sound of the front door open and close even though she knew it was locked; Cathy would then call out, but there was no response. A few minutes later, the door would actually open and her partner Paul would come in. It was almost as though time had jumped ahead and Cathy had anticipated his arrival. Cathy's granddaughter and daughter used to sleep downstairs when they came to stay and on one occasion both of them reported seeing (from the angle they were looking) a foot coming down the stairs.

## An elderly man's appearance

Kathryn Payne has seen the figure of an old man in her house in the High Street. Kath described him as wearing blue trousers and a red sweatshirt top, rather like a gym kit. He apparently walks from the sitting room door to the kitchen door. Kath also reported once hearing the sound of a child crying and said that she knew it was not one of their children; at the time she was playing loud music and the sound of the child was somehow over this.

## Terri Powell and healing

Terri Powell lives at Herston, Swanage, and her paranormal experiences began when she was 4 years old when she saw a ghost in her bedroom at Sandford, near Wareham. She is a psychic lady and now works as a medium, doing readings, leading circles and occasionally 'moving on' troublesome spirits/entities. Terri has engaged in astral travel and healing on occasions. When her father was in hospital following a heart attack, Terri went into a deep meditation and saw herself walking through the hospital corridor in her nightie, even feeling the sensation of the cold floor, and then sitting by her father's bed, where she performed some

*Terri Powell*

healing, with her hands over him, and prayed. The next day her father showed signs of some improvement. One of Terri's sisters said that at the time she was unwell she had a vision of Terri coming through the ceiling, though Terri had not engaged consciously in astral travel.

Terri described another experience relating to healing, which involved her son Daniel, who was in Poole Hospital following a motor bike accident. Daniel had suffered serious injuries to one leg and was given his own room in a ward at the hospital, where Terri stayed with him for 10 days. She practised some psychic healing on Daniel's tibia, where there was a break, and described how she could see blue and green colours emanating from her right hand and had a positive sensation. She did not tell anyone what she had done, but a couple of days later a consultant said the tibia had started to heal itself and that no surgery would be necessary on that part of the leg. Terri sensed the presence of children in the room where Daniel was a patient and both she and a nurse saw a round, grey orb moving between them. The nurse then told Terri that the room was haunted and that badly injured patients (mainly children) were put in that room so they would recover more quickly. A number of patients had apparently reported seeing images of children.

## Burnham's Cross

The T-junction to the south of Godlingston Manor was where a man named Burnham (the lane running westwards from there is known as Burnham's Lane) was buried after hanging himself at his house in Langton Matravers. Reg Saville has informed me that on 13 June 1738 a coroner's inquest held at Langton found that Charles Burnham had taken his own life. Until the late 19th century, a suicide victim could not be interred in consecrated ground but had to be buried at a parish boundary. Burnham was therefore buried at the then parish boundary between Langton Matravers and Swanage

*T-junction, Godlingston*

near Godlingston in the middle of the junction, which became known as Burnham's Cross. There was a grassy mound there for a long time, but this was removed by Dorset County Council.

As a boy I was brought up with the story of Burnham's suicide and how his ghost was supposed to appear on moonlit nights. I cannot say I have ever met anyone who has reported seeing his ghost, but Rachel Helfer who lives at Knitson Old Farmhouse told me that horses were not happy to go past the junction and on one occasion she had a dog that behaved as if terrified. Ilay Cooper, writing in the book *Purbeck Revealed*, reported having uncomfortable feelings around the junction as a young man and disliked having to go past it. Following the demise of many elm trees, the area around there is much more open than it used to be. There is a poem at the end of the book entitled Godlingston Lane which is evocative of the area.

# Langton Matravers

## Knitson Old Farmhouse

Knitson Old Farmhouse nestles snugly against the backdrop of the Purbeck Hills and is close to Nine Barrow Down, the location of Bronze Age burial mounds. Knitson itself lies in the parish of Langton Matravers, though the postal address comes under Corfe Castle. The Old Farmhouse is the home of Rachel Helfer, who has made a very attractive garden which is sometimes open to the public.

One of Rachel's daughters, Rebecca Charron, told me that between the ages of 4 and 10 she regularly saw the ghost of a woman at the farmhouse. Becca's bedroom was in the south wing and during the night she would often get up to go to her parents' bedroom, which involved passing the stairwell. She said that she frequently saw the figure of a lady standing by the stairwell and described her as being slim, quite tall, very upright in appearance and dressed in long, light-coloured clothes. The lady seemed well-turned out and might possibly have been a previous owner. Becca was never frightened of the ghost, but was not entirely comfortable with it. She said that some guests had reported feeling a cold presence in that part of the house. Another of Rachel's daughters, Emily Cable, told me in June 2011 that about once a month she would get the feeling of a presence in the south-facing bedroom, which was quite frightening. She described it as a sudden, unexpected, ice-cold feeling.

## Dairy Cottage

Rebecca Charron lives with her husband Bruno at Dairy Cottage, Knitson, which includes a workshop where Bruno makes wood carvings. In February 1992 one of the oldest parts of the house, thought to date from the early 1700s and originally a barn, underwent considerable renovation when the workshop and an adjoining shop were built. A year or so later Becca recalled going into the shop section and finding one of the carved avocets, which were always placed on a shelf some feet above the ground, standing on the floor in the middle of the room. She thought this was very strange as no one had been in the room. Three months later a very similar incident occurred: Becca unlocked the door and on stepping inside was amazed to find another bird carving standing on the floor in the middle of the room. As before, there was no damage and no one had been into the room to move the carving off the shelf. Becca feels that the renovation work might have disturbed some entity/spirit and that this could, in physical life, have been a youngish person. After the second incident, she would talk out loud to the 'entity' and no further disturbances took place.

## 'Do not have the boy cut!'

This account is about a strange message that was given at a Spiritualist Meeting, which later proved to be correct. Reg Saville, who lives at Langton Matravers, takes up the story:

'When I was aged about five, my maternal grandmother, unknown to my grandfather, had begun to attend Spiritualist Meetings which were held in Swanage on Sunday evenings. Towards the end of the First World War she had lost her only son, to whom she was devoted; he was reported 'Missing, believed killed'. She agonised for several years, wondering if he was still alive, suffering from acute loss of memory and wandering about France, so she had several *Recherches* notices put in French newspapers, but to no avail. So she decided to attend séances to see if she could get a message from him beyond the grave, as this would at least settle the matter as to whether he was indeed dead.

When I was aged eight a fleshy growth known as a 'bursa' came up under my left knee. Within the next year it grew quite large and the family doctor, Dr Rees of Swanage, who was the surgeon at Swanage Hospital, thought that it should be removed surgically, as it would eventually get very large, look unsightly and probably cause a limp. I was therefore booked to go into Swanage Hospital on a certain day. On the Sunday before I was to be admitted to hospital, granny went to the Spiritualist Meeting, where the medium thought to be the best would be appearing. To her great surprise, the medium, after going into a trance, called out, 'Is there anyone here called Polly?' Very excited, thinking that at last she would be getting a message from her son, she called out, 'Yes!' 'Then I have a message for you from Ann' (Ann was the name of her mother-in-law, who had lived with her and her husband during the last 7 years of her life, for three of those years confined to her bed. She had been a rather dictatorial person). The medium continued, 'Ann is *very* insistent that you get this message and act upon it. The message is "Do not have the boy cut!" Do you understand?'

Granny came home and told my mother, but mother, who was sceptical about this alleged interference by her grandmother, was of the opinion that the operation would have to go ahead, as it was all arranged. The following morning Dr Rees arrived. 'Put up your leg!' he ordered. I did so. He shouted, 'You naughty boy, you know that I meant your leg with the bump!' Confused, I put up the other leg. The doctor, now also very confused, felt both knees carefully and then said to my mother, 'I don't understand it. Did you do anything?' She said, 'No, doctor, we have not even looked at it since your last visit.' 'Well, it's completely gone, so he will not have to go to hospital after all.' (It is interesting to note that Reg was not aware himself that the growth had gone when the doctor asked him to put up his leg and he had not been told about the message at the Spiritualist Meeting.)

## A restless spirit?

This story concerns Reg Saville's great-aunt Tilly and paranormal noises in a cottage in Langton Matravers; it took place in 1933.

'My maternal grandmother (the 'Polly' of the previous story) attended Spiritualist Meetings, hoping to get a message from her only son who had been killed in the First World War. By far the best medium at the meetings in Swanage was a lady called Mrs Hallett, who lived in Poole. She sometimes visited my grandmother's home (unknown to grandfather, who would certainly not have approved). I liked Mrs Hallett, for she always treated me as a person in my own right and talked to me, whereas many adults in the 1930s completely ignored children.

I was staying with my grandmother in 1933, as mother was about to give birth to my brother, and when Mrs Hallett came, she and my grandmother planned to visit grandmother's sister Tilly, who lived at the top of the village in a cottage called Trent's. I was told to read a book and that they would be back before long. However, I wanted to go with them and earnestly asked them both to allow this. Eventually, albeit reluctantly on granny's part, I was allowed to go. Apparently, great-aunt Tilly had been unable to sleep because of very loud noises in the night, and when she went downstairs she found that things had been thrown around the room (she had had the experience every night since she moved into the cottage). Granny had suggested that Mrs Hallett should be called in. When Tilly opened the door and Mrs Hallett stepped inside, she shuddered and said, 'Oh, there is a powerful presence here.' Without being told which room was involved, she walked straight into the room on the left and approached the chimney corner, where there was a built-in cupboard. She opened the cupboard, shuddered again and said, 'Please clear out that cupboard completely.' I helped my grandmother and great-aunt and everything was removed, leaving only a wooden shelf half-way up and a large flagstone at the bottom. Mrs Hallett said, 'We must get a crowbar to lift that flagstone', so my great-aunt went to find such a tool. When she returned with a man from next door, we waited whilst he lifted the large stone. Immediately underneath it lay the skeleton of a very small child. The two sisters were horrified, but Mrs Hallett carefully lifted the skeleton, saying, 'Oh, you poor little dear!' and the bones were placed in a cardboard box. 'Now you can put back the stone', she said to the man. He did so. 'And now you can put back all the goods in the cupboard, Mrs Stockting (Tilly), for there will be no more noises or movement of goods to worry you.' She then took the box very reverently to the Rectory, where she requested the clergyman to give the bones Christian burial somewhere. I do not know if there was ever any inquiry about this discovery, but Mrs Hallett was of the opinion that the burial in the cupboard had been done many, many years before. I remember that she thanked me for my help before she left.'

## The little red men in Talbot's Wood

This account, also related by Reg Saville, describes what a 10-year-old boy saw on a walk in 1906 and the possible explanation, which is amazing.

'RJB was born in Langton Matravers in 1896. As a boy aged ten he loved to roam in the fields and woodlands just north of the part of the village where he and his parents lived. The fields were called Twoleas and Cowleaze and the woodland Talbot's Wood. There are two footpaths running through Talbot's Wood, one from south to east and the other from east to west.

When he returned from one such Sunday walk, his mother asked him if he had enjoyed his walk and if he had met anyone. He replied, 'I didn't meet anyone except the little red men, who are always there.' His mother questioned him as to where he saw them and he told her it was on the east to west path in Talbot's Wood. When she asked him what he meant by 'little red men', the boy explained that they were adults, but shorter than most other adult men. They were dressed in long robes of what looked like sack-cloth, which stretched to below their knees. His mother said, 'Well, if they were dressed in sack-cloth, why did you call them 'red'? He replied, 'Oh, it was their hands, faces and legs that were red, not their clothes.' She asked if they spoke at all, and he said that he heard them speaking amongst

*Talbot's Wood*

themselves but he couldn't understand what they said. They ignored him completely and did not even look in his direction.

In those days no one had researched the history of Wilkswood and Talbot's Wood, but when I was told this tale I began researching. I found that Talbot's Wood had been planted by a dairyman called Talbot of Wilkswood Farm in 1816 after the Napoleonic Wars; before that it had been part of the farm Cowleaze. Mr Talbot wanted to 'tidy it up' because there were so many bowl-pits in the land which sloped down steeply to the little stream at its north boundary. I found that the bowl-pits were in fact medieval Purbeck Marble pits, and there was actually a large block of that layer of stone still sitting in the middle of one of the pits. The pits became ponds during the winter months.

I then went further back into the history of Wilkswood and found that it had been a priory of several Benedictine monks during the Middle Ages, known as the Priory of St Leonard, and its function was to look after the lepers of the area. Leprosy died out in England by the 15th century and the little priory then closed, though the farmer who took over the land was still referred to in manorial documents as 'Prior'. The two footpaths are extremely ancient and existed long before the woodland was planted. It is a known fact that the average height of men was shorter in the Middle Ages than in the 20th century. The local dialect of the 13th century would have been very difficult to understand in modern times. The lepers probably used the footpath for daily exercise.' The red colour may be related to the reddish-coloured lesions of leprosy.

## A nebulous ball in Langton Matravers High Street

Reg Saville's mother, Beatrice, also had several paranormal experiences, one of which was the sighting of a nebulous ball in the main street at Langton Matravers. Reg tells the story:

'When walking back from Swanage alone on a dark, cold winter evening about 6 o'clock, when she was aged 16 in 1913, she saw a huge ball, about 30 ft high, rolling down Langton village street on the north pavement. She said that the ball seemed nebulous and to have no weight. (The ball was apparently clearly visible although it was very dark and there were no street lights in those days. She said that it looked like a ball of smoke.) When it reached Cemetery Lane (the green lane leading from the street northwards into Twoleas Meadow), it turned a right-angle and disappeared down that lane. She was terrified and arrived home at Virginia House (the tall, incongruous villa on the south side of the High Street) very shaken. Several weeks later my grandfather learnt that there was a legal row going on between the Anglican and Methodist churches in Langton concerning the ownership of Cemetery Lane, but which the family had not previously heard about.'

## Two ghosts and a poltergeist

A lady who wishes to remain anonymous related to me a series of paranormal experiences that occurred at an old house in Langton Matravers; she will be referred to here by the pseudonym 'Patricia'. The building had been empty for about a year before her family moved in during 1994, and in consequence there was quite a lot of work that needed doing, so the estate agent allowed her to go in before the purchase was completed. She recalled being in the bathroom on the top floor, which is the third storey, when she suddenly heard the front door bang and then footsteps on the wooden stairs (there were no carpets). Assuming that it was the estate agent, she went to investigate, but to her amazement nobody was there.

Approximately 4 years later, Patricia's eldest son, who was 11 at the time and undergoing some emotional stress which left him vulnerable, had a number of frightening experiences in the building. His bedroom was on the second floor near the stairs, part of which was the original very narrow, tight staircase that led up to the third storey, where the attic, which had been turned into a children's playroom, was situated. One summer night he came rushing down the stairs in a very agitated state. It turned out that he had not been in bed as his mother had thought, but had crept up to the attic, which is a large, long room, to watch the tennis on the television. While there, a young girl had appeared in the doorway; he described her as aged between 12 and 14, quite tall, with long hair and wearing a long dress. On making enquiries in the neighbourhood, Patricia discovered from the Rector of Langton that the young girl had reportedly been seen by other people. According to what she was told, the girl was a farmer's daughter who had developed tuberculosis; she was confined to the bedroom in the attic, where she was allowed no visitors, and had died there. Patricia started to call her 'Ellie' and now refers to her as 'Amy', but is not sure why.

Soon after her son had seen the young girl, he started to have very disturbing experiences at night in his bedroom on the second floor. (This room, which is immediately situated above the dining room, has a very old door with a sliding panel, and was possibly where workers were paid from in the past.) Over a period of weeks, his duvet was pulled off many times when he was in bed and on one occasion he even felt that someone (or something) was trying to push him out of the window. Both their dog and cat, which had happily slept in the bedroom, would not do so anymore. It was at that point that the Rector of Langton Matravers came and performed a blessing in the room. The manifestations then ceased in the bedroom and the dog and the cat returned to sleep there.

Several other people had disturbing experiences in the attic when it was used as a bedroom. A friend named Liz came to look after the house while the family was away and brought her two young sons with her. Some years later she wrote a letter to Patricia, describing what had happened. The first night she slept in one of the bedrooms on the second storey and the next morning found the curtains and pole were in a heap on the floor. (Patricia herself had had trouble with curtains in the attic room, having them repeatedly pulled down from their hanger.) On the third night Liz slept in the attic and was very disturbed by what she described as the sound of screaming everywhere. She got up and went down the stairs and stood outside one of her son's rooms; the screaming became so loud that she had to put her hands over her ears. Then she heard a girl's voice, 'If you don't get out, things will be broken'. Everything then went quiet. Despite being terrified, she returned to bed and somehow eventually managed to fall asleep. In the morning she was woken up by her sons running into the attic to tell her that a lot of plates lay broken in the kitchen and they had been woken up by the noise. It was then that Liz decided to leave the house as she believed her children could be at risk; she described the whole experience as 'very traumatic'.

On another occasion Patricia's mother-in-law came to stay and was given the attic bedroom. She unpacked her belongings and put her make-up on the window sill, where a mirror had been placed. When she returned to the room later, she found that her make-up was on the floor and thought it was strange because the door had been shut and the cat could not therefore have got in to disturb anything. That evening they all went out for a meal and on returning the lady again found her make-up on the floor and the mirror moved to the sofa. She then asked, 'Can the cat get in here when the door is closed?' When she was told there was no way the cat could have gained entry and that 'the ghost' might have been responsible for moving items, she immediately asked for another room. It is also of interest that on two or three other occasions Patricia found the mirror moved to different locations in the attic room.

Patricia decided to try an experiment in which she placed six ping-pong balls with faces drawn on them in a line next to the mirror on the attic window sill at night to see if anything would happen. Whenever she did this and then checked the balls the following morning, she would find they had moved from their original positions; the strange thing was that sometimes the one in the middle had moved out of line into the corner. She stressed that the window was always closed on these occasions and there did not appear to be a draught.

Regarding the young girl who had been seen in the attic, a psychic friend of Patricia's came and brought with her a crystal on a chain. The friend was standing at one end of the kitchen holding the crystal steady and Patricia was sitting down by the table and told to ask questions; if the answer were 'yes', the crystal would move in a circle, and if the answer were 'no', the movement would be backwards and forwards. She first asked if there was a young girl haunting the building, and the way the crystal moved suggested an affirmative answer. When she then asked if the girl liked her son, the crystal spun around violently, snapped off the chain and flew about 12 ft across the room, where it hit the stone wall and smashed.

Other paranormal phenomena were recorded in the house, including the dining room, which is the oldest part of the building and dates to 1710, with ships' timbers in the ceiling. A previous owner's daughter said she had seen a man's figure in the dining room on several occasions, which made Patricia wonder if that was why her younger son had an aversion to playing the piano in that room. There was also the occasion when a pile of piano music books had disappeared and then mysteriously reappeared years later on top of the piano. She questioned her younger son carefully about this, but it was clear from his reaction that he was not responsible. Her art portfolio also reappeared on top of the bookshelf on the stairs after being 'lost' for about 5 years. On another occasion, a book on how to give up smoking disappeared from the same bookshelf, only to reappear a few months later on top of some magazines in the kitchen. Patricia also took a number of photographs inside the building with her digital camera, which show orbs; some of these photographs are of people and others of empty rooms. No orbs have appeared on pictures in recent years, yet she still has the same camera.

Furthermore, Patricia described a run of 'bad luck' that had affected her family for a number of years, involving accidents and serious health problems. She believes it was far more than 'coincidence' and that it was related to what was happening in the building. She then asked Liz, the friend who had had such dramatic experiences when she came with her two young sons to stay, if she could help as she appeared to be psychically gifted. Liz 'visited' the house through astral travel and said the focus of the problem was a poltergeist located in the study near the ceiling. Interestingly, Patricia had often had an uneasy feeling herself when sitting at the computer in that room, with the urge to glance upwards towards an oak beam; the thought had even occurred to her that someone might have hanged himself/herself from it. Liz also saw the girl (mostly in the attic) and the man (she called George) standing in the dining room facing the wall; these ghosts, according to her, were unrelated to the poltergeist and were even trying to protect the family from it. Patricia, it should be noted, had not told Liz about the two ghosts prior to this. Liz worked on the house through her spiritual gift (certain ceremonies were performed in the building as well) to remove the poltergeist. Eventually, the negative energy was cleared and Patricia describes the atmosphere now as normal. The poltergeist seems to have gone, but Liz believes the two ghosts are still there. Patricia's mother-in-law is now happy to sleep in the attic and the last orb to show on a photograph was in December 2007. The main paranormal activity had taken place between 1998 and 2007.

The interesting question is why no paranormal activity apparently occurred between Patricia's initial experience and her son's dramatic experiences 4 years later. Was there some kind of catalyst? Patricia did tell me that prior to her son's experiences, the ouija board had been used several times. On one notable occasion, she, her two sons, and a friend and her son were using the board; the visiting boy was quite sceptical and said he wanted to speak to his deceased grandfather. The board spelled out 'cigar case' and the boy visibly paled: his mother then said his grandfather had been shot during the war and the position of the cigar case he had been carrying saved his life. At a later date, they were using the ouija board again and it spelled out some very abusive language in an aggressive manner; Patricia then decided that they would not do anymore dabbling and she thinks this was about a year before her son started having his paranormal experiences. It is possible, therefore, that dabbling with the ouija board may have triggered the poltergeist activity in the house, though Patricia's eldest son's emotional state may have been a factor.

## Roger Smith and the Ship Inn

Roger Smith has been the landlord of the Ship Inn, situated in the High Street, Langton Matravers, since 2008. Readers may be interested to know that the original Ship Inn was next door, but, following the suicide of the landlord John Ball inside the pub in 1878, it was decided to rebuild it. As was the custom with suicides at that time, John's body was buried at night in a field in an unmarked grave. The Rector

*Roger Smith*

of Langton Matravers felt that this law was so unjust that he successfully started a campaign to have it changed so that suicide victims could be given a Christian burial. John's wife Mary was the sister of Syndonia Stevens, who features in Chapter 3.

Roger, who doesn't live at the pub but in a village in Purbeck, has not so far encountered anything paranormal in the modern Ship Inn, but has had a number of interesting experiences in different locations in Britain. His first experience came as a boy when he attended the Royal Wansted School at Snaresbrook and after his father had been killed. One night he woke up freezing cold and felt a definite evil presence. As he looked across the room, he could make out the misty shape of his father and felt that he was protecting him from the presence. The following morning he overheard a conversation in the dormitory in which a German boy was describing how he had seen a misty figure in the night in the same place that Roger had seen it. The school was apparently used as an Italian prisoner of war camp in the Second World War.

It would seem that Roger is used to haunted pubs. Before taking over the Ship Inn, he and his wife Sue ran the Carpenter Arms at Wick near Bath, which had a reputation for being haunted. On the third day after they moved in, Roger caught a glimpse of a lady sitting on the settee in the lounge; she had a smile on her face, as if in welcome. The locals later told him that she was the ghost of a previous landlady who had run the pub for about 40 years and then bought a bungalow 30 yards away, where she had died 6 months later. On another occasion, Roger was serving in the pub when there was only one customer. A voice distinctly said, 'Do you two want a drink?' According to locals, it was the same ghost and previous landlords had apparently experienced this often. Roger's mother, who had not previously been aware of any paranormal activity, came to stay at the pub and witnessed a little old lady standing at the foot of her bed, whom she described as wearing lacy farm clothes and a hat. Roger also reported how they would be sitting in the lounge and their dog would appear to be watching something going past towards the kitchen and not looking towards the people in the lounge.

## The King's Arms

A former landlady at the King's Arms, Langton Matravers, described how the pub had originally been two cottages and at one time the front room on the east side was used as a mortuary, with the one on the west being run as a doctor's surgery. The room used as a mortuary has a reputation for being icy cold, which was confirmed by Tim Cattle, who used to be a customer at the pub.

A ghost known as 'George', dressed in a trench coat, was allegedly seen by a previous landlord, while a group of locals sitting in the back room apparently saw a man coming up to the bar, who then vanished. Rachael Aplin also reported that on one occasion when she was there, she had seen a figure walking from the kitchen to the front room.

## Capstan Fields

When I spoke to Pippa Cattle in her house at Capstan Fields, Langton Matravers, one day in early December 2011, she told me she had lived there with her children for nearly 4 years. The property was built around 1948 and had been owned by the same family until Pippa moved in. She said that she sometimes feels a presence, mostly upstairs and especially on the landing, and once saw a man with a moustache standing at the top of the stairs. She has heard footsteps upstairs and also bangs, as if someone has dropped something.

## Farmer Cull and the noise at the cottage

I am grateful to Reg Saville for the following story. 'Farmer Cull', as he was always called, had a local reputation for 'great wickedness'. There is a legend that when he died, he was not buried because the devil came and carried him off on account of the fact that he was one of his most loyal servants!

'In Garfield Lane, Langton Matravers, there is a cottage called Cull's. In the early 20th century the villagers called it Black House because its north wall, which faced the village, was painted with pitch because it was always damp. The occupants were Farmer Cull's widow and her two daughters (hence the later name of the cottage).

When Mrs Cull died, her daughters moved away and the house was put up for rent. Two families successively went there to live, but each stayed only a few days, claiming that the noises in the night were so loud and frightening that they could not sleep. The house then lay empty for some years.

Eventually, two young men of Langton Matravers, George Corben and his friend William Crocker, made a bet in the King's Arms that they would not be afraid to sleep there for an entire night. They took a pile of bedding and moved in. In the morning they left, having won the bet, but shortly thereafter they both bought their passage to Australia, much to the amazement of their families, who had no idea where the money for such a venture had come from. They never revealed this, but local folk believed that they had followed the sound of the noises that night and dug up Farmer Cull's money which had been hidden by him under the flagstones of his cottage. A little later a newly appointed local schoolmaster, Mr George Reed, took over the house, as it was very near the school, renamed it Vectis View (because the Isle of Wight, which the Romans called Vectis, could be seen from the bedroom windows) and he and Mrs Reed lived there quite happily for many years, without any noises ever troubling them.'

## Charles Hayward's monument

The following account from Reg Saville concerns the centenary celebration of the rebuilding of St George's Church, Langton Matravers. The church was rebuilt in 1876 after the appearance of cracks in the ceiling, thought to have been caused by the hiding of smuggled tubs of brandy. The principal smuggler was the local churchwarden, Charles Hayward.

'In 1976 St George's Parish Church in Langton Matravers celebrated the 100th anniversary of its rebuilding. I wrote a Pageant of the History of Langton Church to celebrate the occasion. It was performed on a large stage at the west end of the building against the ancient wall and all the chairs were turned around to face west. Obviously, the penultimate scene had to be the declaration of the previous building as unsafe and the contributory reasons for that, so an actor representing Charles Hayward appeared on stage with his grandson Charlie Dean, and then two other men carrying barrels appeared. As this happened there was a tremendously loud clap of thunder and all the lights went out. The fuse had been blown and we all sat in darkness whilst a soprano and a tenor from my choir sang some songs by light of a torch. As soon as the lights came on again, we hurried to complete the eleventh and twelfth scenes of the pageant and then everyone went home. There was no rain, no further thunder and no further lightning until 2 a.m. when a very severe thunderstorm took place.

At 9 o'clock the next morning I went to the church to dismantle the stage and curtains and to put back the chairs. I discovered that Charles Hayward's monument in Purbeck stone and Purbeck marble had fallen from the north wall and lay shattered on the floor. His descendant, John Dean from Swanage, took all the pieces and reassembled the monument and fixed it very securely in its original position. It can be seen, with cracks and two tiny pieces missing (which had gone down through the floor boards) on the north wall between the doors into the vestry and the organ screen. I could not help wondering if the former churchwarden, parish clerk and postmaster had been annoyed at our portrayal of him on stage and had responded by causing his monument to leap down and shatter!'

It does seem a remarkable coincidence that it was this monument that fell down after the enactment of the pageant, which had depicted Charles Hayward as a smuggler.

# Band practice in an old cottage

Paranormal activity has been recorded at this very old cottage in Langton. The first account was told to Reg Saville by an American professor who used to stay each year at the cottage with his wife and son; following what happened, they did not stay there again.

'One night at about 2 a.m. the professor's wife awoke to find that her husband was not in the bed beside her. She called to him, but there was no reply. As the landing light was switched on, she got up, put on her dressing gown and slippers and went out onto the landing. She found all the lights had been switched on downstairs, so she went down, calling her husband's name. The back door of the cottage stood wide open, but there was no one near. Then, in the dim light made by the downstairs lights, she thought she could see someone at the very end of the long garden, where there was a hedge. She took a torch and went down the garden, which was all lawn, and found her husband standing right in the hedge with his hands over his ears. When he saw her, he said, 'Have they gone? Has the noise stopped?' She told him that there was no one but herself on the premises and that it was quite quiet. 'Thank God!' he cried, and gingerly walked back to the cottage with her. However, he would not go to bed again, but they sat up talking and drinking until it was daylight. Then they packed and left for America.

He had been awakened that night by the sounds of a brass band playing at close quarters, with some of the instruments playing out of tune or making wrong notes. He immediately got up, put on some clothes and went downstairs. In the living room the noise was deafening, but he could see no cause for it. Eventually, he fled down the garden as far as he could to get away from the raucous sounds. He said that the experience was very frightening.

When he told me, I remembered that Mrs Serrell, the eccentric widow of Durnford Manor House (who owned it in the 19th century), had made a band practice room on her property, but as far away from the house as possible. Her band had been allowed to practise in this cottage, where no one would hear the dreadful noise they would obviously have to make in order to learn to play their instruments.'

It is interesting to learn that the band eventually became very good and four of their instruments can be seen in Langton Matravers Museum.

There is another story related to the same cottage that appears in Olive Knott's book *Dorset Again*. The story concerns a gentleman farmer who had married a village girl, but they were not happy together and the husband would sometimes throw cold water in his wife's face. The woman, getting tired of the abuse, visited Jenny Gould, a local wise woman who lived in

Studland. Jenny told her that the next time her husband threw water into her face, she was to ask him about the cottage.

After seeing that her husband was moved by the mention of the cottage, the girl returned to Jenny Gould to find out what he had done. 'Come again in a month's time', she was told. Exactly a month later the man fell from a load of hay and broke his neck. His wife went straight to Jenny and was told that her husband had murdered his aunt and buried her body at the cottage. It was said that for some time afterwards the cottage was haunted by the woman's ghost and the rustle of her silk dress could be heard at nightfall.

Jenny Gould lived in a cottage between Ulwell (north Swanage) and Studland, close to the road junction that leads to Currendon Hill. She was regarded as a witch, but was also helpful to the local smugglers, who would store hundreds of tubs of smuggled liquor in the cellar of her cottage after hauling them up the cliffs at Ballard Head and then transporting them across the downs. I have been unable to obtain a reliable date for Jenny Gould, or this story relating to the cottage at Langton, but late 18th/early 19th century is probable.

# Harmans Cross

## Psychic impressions from the past

Pippa Cattle related several experiences that she had had at a property in Harmans Cross, where she lived from the age of 12–17, roughly 1995–2000. She shared the front bedroom with her sister and said she had regularly felt that someone was sitting on her bed just before she fell asleep and that she thought it was her great grandfather. There was also sometimes the smell of talcum powder, such as her great grandmother might have used. Tim, Pippa's father, told me that he could sometimes smell cigarette smoke there.

One night Pippa had a dream in which her great grandmother was standing in the middle of the empty bedroom; she was wearing a brown knee-length skirt and a yellow blouse and was holding a baby. The dream occurred on 14 October, the anniversary of her great grandmother's death, and the room in the dream was exactly how it was in reality when Pippa was using it. Pippa's aunt had been born in that bedroom and her father was very moved by her dream as he had been close to his nan.

By a strange coincidence (or synchronicity?) I nearly bought this property myself some years ago and 14 October is the anniversary of my mother's death.

# Chapter 2

# Paranormal Activity in the Corfe Castle and Wareham Areas

This chapter contains paranormal accounts from the central, western and northern parts of Purbeck, covering Kingston, Creech, Tyneham, Corfe Castle, Rempstone, Norden and Wareham.

## Kingston

### 'Grandma Bartlett' at the Scott Arms

The Virginia Creeper-clad Scott Arms is a well-known country pub situated on the hill at Kingston, with a commanding view northwards to Corfe Castle, the Purbeck Hills and Poole Harbour. The pub takes its name from a local family that used to own the Encombe estate and the building dates to the late 18th century; there are two bars, dining areas and an extensive garden at the back, which is often full on busy days in the season.

When I spoke to three of the bar staff in May 2011, all of them mentioned the figure of a woman (known as 'Grandma Bartlett') who has been seen by at least several people. Barman Jamie Bartlett (not a relative) said that he had gone into the north bar one winter's evening when it was closed and the lights were out and had seen the figure of an old woman in white going out of the door into the corridor; he experienced a definite tingling in the spine and felt he had 'disturbed' something. When he returned to the top bar, the locals said, 'You look like you've seen a ghost!' On occasions others have experienced strange feelings in the north bar and also the kitchen, and various people have mentioned seeing the figure of a woman, including someone reporting her sitting on the seat upstairs, which is part of the north bar. Jamie also said that one member of staff had run down the stairs looking frightened and pale; she had apparently encountered a figure in white in one of the upstairs rooms while making the bed.

Local resident Stephen Coleman related a disconcerting experience that had occurred to him in the early 1990s when he was working in the pub. It was early one morning before the pub had opened and he had been doing

*Scott Arms, Kingston*

various jobs, such as cleaning out the fires. He then went on to describe how he had been walking behind the main bar and suddenly felt a definite pinch on his bottom. As there was no one else there at the time, it came as quite a surprise!

Barman Geoff Dennis remembered a young couple sitting in the small room adjoining the north bar: the man came over to say that his girlfriend felt there was paranormal activity going on and the young man then asked if there were any ghosts. The current landlord, Ian Coppack, has been there since 2009 and has not experienced anything himself, though a previous landlord apparently did and was able to show people a picture of 'Grandma Bartlett'. The censuses of 1891 and 1901 both record a family by the name of Bartlett running the pub, which was called the Eldon Arms in those days.

# Creech

## Creech Grange: Norman Hayward and the ghost dog

Creech Grange stands in a picturesque and peaceful setting just to the north of the Purbeck Hills and a few miles south of Wareham. It was built by Sir Oliver Lawrence, an ancestor of George Washington, in the 16th century and bought by Nathaniel Bond in 1691, whose family then owned it for 300 years. As well as the elegant Grange, there is a chapel, outhouses and 300 acres of land. Norman Hayward, the present owner, described several unusual experiences relating to what may have been a ghost dog.

*Creech Grange*

Norman bought the Grange in the early 1980s and not long afterwards started to let several cottages, one of which is known as The Courtyard. He related how a rather strange lady had come to stay for a week, who said that she could see a number of ghosts and would walk around patting a 'ghost dog', which no one else could see. Sometime later, foster children stayed there for several years and also a dog called Buster. After the children had left, Buster was kept on. Then, a family, including a girl suffering from paralysis, rented the cottage and Buster was very friendly towards them. The disabled girl needed to be lifted onto the toilet and one day she mentioned that Buster had come to see her while she was there, which seemed very strange as he had been somewhere else at the time. The next day a similar thing happened, with the girl saying she had seen Buster on the landing, when he was elsewhere.

One year later Norman was decorating the cottage and happened to pull away some wallpaper. To his amazement, written in pencil on the wall were the words: 'There is a ghost dog in this room'. There was a strange sequel to this when a school for pupils with learning disabilities visited the Grange: one group was making a video up on the stairs and the inevitable question about whether the Grange had any ghosts was asked. As Norman started to relate the story of the ghost dog, a real dog actually barked twice, making the group jump with surprise!

# Tyneham

## The phantom army

Perhaps the most famous old ghost story from Purbeck, and one of the most curious, is that of the phantom army, which was seen in December

1678 by Captain John Laurence of Creech Grange and witnessed by more than 100 other people. The army was said to number several thousand and was seen to march from Flower's Barrow (near Tyneham) along the Purbeck Hills. Interestingly, it was only seen from the north side of the hill. A full account is given by local historian, the Rev. John Hutchins, in his *History and Antiquities of the County of Dorset* (Volume 1). Hutchins based most of his account on what he had gleaned from Thomas Bolt, a resident of Wareham, who had probably spoken to eyewitnesses. The sighting of the 'army' was so realistic that 300 militia were marched to Wareham and the bridge barricaded. Captain Laurence and his brother hurried to London to inform the government (the possibility of invasion was uppermost in people's minds at the time), yet nothing more was seen of the army.

It is clear that Hutchins was incredulous and dismissive regarding the sighting, attributing it to 'the thick fogs and mists that often hang on the hills in Purbeck', yet, as other authors have commented before, are we seriously to believe that in excess of 100 eyewitnesses, all with local knowledge of the weather, got confused into thinking that there was an army as a result of unusual shapes made by mist? We do not even know what the weather was like on that day. What about the 'great noise and clashing of arms' that was supposed to have been heard? That certainly cannot be attributed to Purbeck mist! Captain Laurence, too, must have been well aware of the penalties for false alarm, particularly at a time of political upheaval.

There have been more recent reports of a possible phantom army and some say that it is formed of Roman soldiers. Flower's Barrow may have been defended against a Roman army, but it has not been comprehensively excavated (part of it has fallen into the sea) and there is no historical evidence that a Roman army ever marched in Purbeck. It would seem from Hutchins' account that the army seen in 1678 was not recognised as a phantom and there is no talk of Roman soldiers. On the day that it was

*Povington Hill from Tyneham—the phantom army reportedly marched along this hill.*

seen it was clearly regarded as a real threat to the country and therefore as something contemporary. Could it perhaps have been a phantom army from a more recent period, such as the Civil War (1642–49)? Spectral armies have been reported from different parts of Britain as well as other countries, one of the most famous being Edgehill in Warwickshire, where local people reported seeing the re-enactment of the bloody battle of 1642 between the Cavalier and Roundhead armies. King Charles I sent four officers to investigate and they saw the phantom army themselves, even recognising some of their dead comrades!

## Worbarrow Bay: a smuggler's death

The Isle of Purbeck saw considerable smuggling activity during the 18th and early 19th centuries, with contraband goods being landed at a number of suitable bays and cliffs all along the coast. Coastguard stations, including one at Worbarrow Bay, were established to deter the smugglers and violent clashes between the preventive men and smugglers sometimes occurred.

One such incident, mentioned in Llewellyn Pridham's book *The Dorset Coastline*, seems to have taken place on the beach at Worbarrow Bay near the village of Tyneham, which is now a ruin. The story goes that a smuggler was pursued along the beach by the revenue men to where he could go no further, having come up against the sheer cliff face. The desperate man then jumped into the sea to try to escape, but was stoned to death by his pursuers. According to Pridham, it is said that on certain nights the sounds of the struggle can still be heard, including half-choked screams.

*Worbarrow Bay*

No one has lived at Worbarrow Bay or Tyneham since 1943, following the requisition of the area by the Army in that year for military training purposes. Public access is at weekends and school holidays, with the gate leading down to the village being closed at night. It is therefore unlikely that any recent paranormal activity will have been recorded, though a fisherman I spoke to was aware of the story. Tyneham itself is often referred to as a 'ghost village' and most of the remaining buildings are ruined; interesting displays on the history of the village can be seen in the church and the old school room.

# Corfe Castle

## The Castle Inn

The Castle Inn, which is a Grade 2 listed building, is situated in East Street, Corfe Castle, and is a few minutes' walk from the village centre, in contrast to its three rivals which are located near the busy square.

Tracy Brown, who works in the National Trust Shop, has lived in the village since the late 1980s , and when I spoke to her in December 2011 she told me that her stepfather, Gordon Greer, ran the Castle Inn in the early

*Castle Inn, Corfe Castle*

1990s. She said that sometimes he would be sitting in the bar late at night and would hear footsteps above him moving to and fro. There was also one occasion when someone was pushed over near the dart board, which could not be accounted for. Tracy worked there herself in about 2001 and recalled that the dog appeared to sense something near the wall by the fireplace next to the gents, as it would bark in that area with its hackles rising.

Laurice Turner, the landlady of the Castle since 2006, has not experienced anything herself, but, according to her, one of the barmaids has seen the figure of a lady walking across the bar room a number of times. Debbie Reynolds, who also works in the National Trust Shop, related a disconcerting incident that had occurred to her father one winter's night in the early 1980s when he was delivering some football pools to the pub: as he opened the main door and went inside, he felt a sharp slap on his face. At the time, renovation work was being done to a fireplace in the bar and paranormal activity is often associated with disturbance to buildings. Laurice said that she had been told that a workman had once had his face slapped in a room upstairs when there had been no one there. Could it be that the ghost has an aversion to men?

## Corfe Fields

When Tracy Brown was working at the Castle Inn in about 2001, she would sometimes take a short cut to the village centre by walking past Abbots Cottages and through the fields. She recalled that on a number of occasions she saw a dark shape near the top of the hill in the field moving along at the same speed as herself. Her father also saw the shape when he was with her,

*Corfe fields*

as did her boyfriend another time: the latter was so scared that he ran off. Another spooky sighting, which may be related to the above, occurred in the same area in May 2009, an account of which appeared in the *Bournemouth Daily Echo*. Local fisherman Don Goodwin was out in the early hours of the morning collecting worms for bait when he saw a ghostly figure of a man in the middle of the field. He described the figure as tall and he saw it move as if to pick something up. The man was wearing a long cloak with a very high collar and a small, floppy-browed hat, which made him look like a cavalier. Don bent down to pick up more worms and as he got back up, the figure vanished.

## The Greyhound Inn

The Greyhound Inn is situated at the heart of Corfe Castle and is undoubtedly one of the most photographed pubs in Britain, with the ruined castle forming the imposing backdrop to most pictures. Ralph Treswell's map of 1586 shows two separate detached properties on the site (the middle section of the present property was added later); some of the earliest stonework in the pub may have come from the ruined castle. The name of the pub could be derived from the King's Messengers, who were denoted by the symbol of a silver greyhound, originating at the time of Charles II's exile: the King broke four silver greyhounds attached to a bowl and gave them to four trusted men, each of whom was to take a message to the Royalist forces in England.

Barmaid Sue Barnes spoke to me in May 2011 and said she had lived in the pub for 5 years, during which a number of paranormal phenomena had occurred, particularly about 2 years previously. She described alarms going off at night of their own volition, objects projecting themselves at people, and her own feeling when sitting in the pub of the atmosphere changing with lots of people around. On one occasion, Sue and a customer were sitting in the bar and could hear the sound of barrels rolling across the floor above the ceiling on the east side of the pub (barrels had originally been stored up there); she said that the pub was like a time warp.

The ghost of a man known as 'Henry' has apparently been seen and is described as wearing an old-fashioned tunic. One night the figure of a man was seen by two local customers: one sighting was in the gents and the other was of the man walking near the main door. Sue said the activity seemed centred around the west side of the pub and near the toilets. In November 2012 Sue told me that several customers had reported seeing ghosts in recent months in the same area and she described her own feeling on one occasion of a definite presence near the toilets when it was like

*Greyhound Inn, Corfe Castle*

'hitting a brick wall'. She said she was also aware of shapes out of the corner of her eye and sometimes felt as if two worlds were colliding in the pub.

One customer told me he had lived in the pub a few years ago and had been aware of paranormal activity, in particular small objects flying off the shelves, especially in relation to one man who had been working in the pub. A man I spoke to subsequently at the King's Arms, Stoborough, said that he had been doing some work at the Greyhound a few years before and recalled that there had been talk of paranormal phenomena and how objects had been flying around.

Jacci Pestana, who has owned the Greyhound since 2000, related her experiences to me in November 2011. She said she had seen the ghostly figure of a woman on two occasions. She described how the first week they moved into the pub, she saw the figure of a woman in a long grey cape at the west side of the bar; she could tell it was a woman by the way the figure moved. On the next occasion, she saw the woman first on the CCTV camera in the bar before actually seeing her in the bedroom; the figure was again dressed in a long grey cape and Jacci described her as having long dark hair and very red lips. She also mentioned how several guests who had stayed in the pub experienced the feeling of pressure on their chests. A 'cleansing' ceremony took place in the back room of the pub a few years ago, since when there has been less activity.

# The headless woman

There have been several reports of a ghostly figure of a headless woman at Corfe Castle. Myrtle Grace lived in Brook Cottage, East Street, in the early 1970s and, according to Rachael Aplin, is reported to have seen it near to where the drawbridge of the castle would have been. Perhaps the best known account was given by local resident John Seager, which appeared in the *Swanage Times* 12 July 1967. John had been driving his van towards the mill above the bridge early one morning when he suddenly saw a figure in front of him; as he drew nearer, he braked hard. The paper reported him as saying:

'There it was, a white figure, headless, and seemingly wearing a long nightgown, drifting across the road in front of me. It moved on and down the path at the foot of the castle hill near the bakery. I trembled and came over cold; in fact, I felt frozen. It was an experience I would never want again.'

When John recounted his experience to a number of people at the Bankes Arms, Corfe Castle, there was some scepticism expressed and he then said he thought something bad would happen if they did not believe him. A few minutes after the bar had closed and the customers had left, the ceiling above the room where he had been describing his experience collapsed, sending down plaster and rubble, a picture of which also appeared in the *Swanage Times*.

According to websites, the headless woman may have been seen again in 1976 and 1993. There is speculation as to who she may have been, but it is not likely to have been Lady Mary Bankes (the defender of the castle against parliamentary forces during the Civil War), as some have suggested, because she never lost her head and died peacefully at Kingston Lacy.

# Brook Cottage

Jasmine Cattle and her family lived at Brook Cottage in East Street for about 13 years from 1987. The cottage dates to about 1730 and is currently used as a holiday let. The property consists of three storeys and there is one bedroom at the top, to which they added a bathroom, where Jasmine could sometimes smell lavender perfume. Two of Jasmine's sons shared the bedroom and both reported hearing the sound of footsteps coming up the stairs as far as the bedroom door. Tim also said that he could sometimes hear door latches moving. Jasmine did some bed and breakfast at Brook Cottage and remembered several visitors asking if there were ghosts as they could sense something; the feeling was always positive as there was

*Boar Mill below Corfe Castle; paranormal activity has been reported from several locations in this area.*

no apparent threat. Jasmine's husband, Trevor, said that he had never experienced anything himself during the time they lived there. The current owners have also not experienced any paranormal phenomena.

## Property in East Street

Jasmine Cattle's youngest son, Patrick, lived with his wife Corrinne in a house in East Street from about 1991–2004. They said it had a very strange atmosphere and they witnessed the lid of an indoor waste bin shifting of its own volition, as well as cutlery moving. They kept several cats and both Jasmine and her husband Trevor remember how they would all move very quickly to get out of the kitchen through the cat flap as though something had frightened them. Eventually, Patrick and Corrinne asked someone to come and remove the paranormal activity. This person told them that she felt a young soldier, who had been imprisoned in the castle, had escaped and been killed and also that a young boy had got out of the castle too, but had fallen by the garden wall and broken his leg, with the result that he was unable to escape. They were told to burn a candle every night for 14 days; this was duly carried out, but when Corrinne's father once came in to check on the candle, he found it was burning at both ends! He was unable to explain this and, feeling thoroughly disconcerted, left hurriedly.

# Rempstone

## Rempstone Hall

Rempstone Hall is in an isolated location, set back from the Corfe Castle to Studland road. The name Rempstone could have several possible derivations, but may well come from the Old English 'Hring-Stun', which means 'stone circle'. This could therefore refer to the stone circle that is situated not far from the Hall and believed to have been erected in the Bronze Age, approximately 4,000 years ago. It is now partly enclosed by woodland but is visited by a number of people, some of whom place coins, shells or flowers on the stones, and is quite an atmospheric site.

During the late 18th century Rempstone Hall was considerably enlarged from the original 17th century building and was owned by the Calcraft family at that time. Some paranormal activity has been reported and it is said that the ghost of Lady Caroline Calcraft, described as a religious fanatic, haunts the Hall. Guy Marston owned the Hall from 1901–27 and was friendly with the occultist Aleister Crowley, who performed ritualistic magic there. It is possible that Crowley's dabbling led to paranormal disturbances, and at least one exorcism has taken place.

Rempstone Hall is currently owned by James Ryder, and his daughter Lara Manningham-Buller now lives there. Although she has not experienced anything herself, she told me:

'More recently there have been the usual ghostly sightings or feelings reported by various occupiers of the house, but probably no more than in any other house with 17th century origins. I do remember that a friend of my father arranged for a group of people to visit the house about 10 or 15 years ago to feel for any spirits and they found a couple of presences which they found very interesting. I am not sure if they performed an exorcism or whether it was alleged to have been many years earlier.'

# Norden

## St Edward's Cottage

I visited St Edward's Cottage, Norden, with Rachael Aplin in early February 2012. It was a bitterly cold morning, but the tenant of the cottage, Angela Waterman, made us very welcome, as did her Labrador dog, Millie. The cottage and land are owned by the National Trust and used to form part of the Bankes Estate. Angela believes that parts of the present building may date to the 17th century; straw has been found under some of the floor boards, which would indicate some antiquity. The land at the back is known as Gallows Hill and was presumably the site of a gallows in former times. There is a well with a stone surround in the garden.

St Edward's Cottage has been associated with the murder of King Edward the Martyr in 978 and subsequent alleged miraculous events. King Edward was assassinated at Corfe Castle on the orders of his stepmother, Elfrida, who wanted her own son, Ethelred, on the throne. After his murder, it is recorded that Edward's body was taken to the cottage of a blind woman; a strange light appeared in the cottage the following night and the old lady found she could see. Elfrida, who was frightened by this account, ordered the body to be hidden in a nearby well, where it remained for a year. When the body was discovered, it is said that a brilliant ray of light illuminated the spot; the body was supposedly intact and the water pure. The well became known as St Edward's Fountain and was visited by the sick, hoping for a cure. The exact location of the blind woman's cottage and well is not known, but it is possible that St Edward's Cottage may have been built over the site of the original cottage (though it could have been at Corfe Castle itself). It is said that people used to call at St Edward's Cottage to ask for the miracle water. By a strange coincidence (synchronicity?) Angela Waterman is herself partially sighted and her husband's name was Edward. Perhaps the synchronicity is continued in the name 'Waterman'.

*St Edward's Cottage, Norden*

Angela told us that her mother had married the previous tenant, Don Basket, a herdsman, in 1996. She herself had then come to live at the cottage with her late husband, Edward, around the year 2002. Angela went on to describe how Edward, who had been fairly sceptical of the paranormal, had seen the ghost of a lady a few years later in his bedroom downstairs, which is located opposite the lounge. He was lying in bed at the time and saw the figure of an elderly lady in a crinoline nightdress floating across the room from the door and disappear through the window. The description of 'floating' may be an indication that the room was originally at a different level. Angela said that she can sometimes see lights in the corner of her bedroom upstairs and the shape of the room appears to have changed. She also hears latches lifting and knocking on the window, but the feeling she gets inside the cottage is one of friendliness and there is nothing unpleasant. While we were walking around, Rachael felt that the bedroom downstairs had the most psychic atmosphere, but she also experienced something half-way down the stairs and felt that a passage or room might once have existed on the west side.

A friend of Angela's, Brian, was present when we first arrived. He walks the dog for Angela and told us that Millie does not like walking between the fence and the stream near the bus stop. Apparently, a serious accident occurred there and it is possible that the dog can sense this.

## The lady with the primroses

Cherry and Alf Stearn used to live at Norden Farm and Cherry recalled a strange experience that had happened to her in around 1975. Early one morning, as she was walking along the lane near Norden Bridge, she saw a lady coming towards her. This lady was dressed rather old-fashionedly in a long, grey flannelled skirt, cape and bonnet, and on her arm she was carrying a basket full of primroses. As they passed each other, the lady said, 'Mornin'. It was only after she had gone by that the thought struck Cherry that the lady's basket should have contained blackberries, not primroses, as it was September!

A neighbour later told her there had once been a shepherd's hut in the wood nearby that had burnt down. 'Perhaps the woman you saw was the shepherd's wife', the neighbour suggested. Cherry also spoke to a lady living on Norden Heath who said she could never ride her horse down that lane but had to lead it, as it was too frightened; she herself also found the lane spooky.

# Wareham

## The Quay Inn

The Quay Inn, conveniently located close to the South Bridge at Wareham, dates back to 1747 when it was called the Shovel and the Crown; in 1930 it was renamed the New Inn and in 1988 it was given its present name. Paul and Sue Brenson, who run the pub, first spoke to me in December 2011 when they had been there for 2 years. They were aware of paranormal activity about 3 weeks after they moved in, sometimes hearing footsteps in the corridor upstairs when there was no one there.

Paul told me about a number of strange incidents that have occurred, including the sensation of having his shirt tugged when he was standing by the entertainment board left of the bar, seeing what appears to be people out of the corner of his eye, his 3-year-old grandson speaking about a little boy upstairs, and barmaids reporting glasses falling off the shelf in the bar and moving half-way across the bar. He described how he was once in the kitchen with Ceri, a member of staff, and saw what appeared to be water drip on her head, but on carefully examining the ceiling for leaks, found that it was completely dry. A couple of locals have reported seeing an old lady in front of the fire near the door and one of Paul's dogs seems to sense something around that area. Paul said that before they took over the pub, a barmaid had once reported a man dressed in First World War uniform who had come into the pub and said he was waiting for his sweetheart. He went and sat over in the corner, but was never seen again.

*Quay Inn, Wareham*

Andy Pethick used to work in the kitchen. He told me that he did not believe in the paranormal until one day he felt himself being pushed in the back when there was no one there. He also witnessed a butter knife flying out of the butter.

Vickie Walters has been working as a barmaid at the Quay Inn since about 2007. She described how several years ago she would regularly see the black shape of a man out of the corner of her eye as she was coming from the cellar into the bar. The figure would pass the archway as if it had come from the direction of the main door and Vickie would walk forward to the end of the bar to serve whom she presumed was a customer, only to find that there was no one there. This experience would sometimes occur once or twice a week at different times of the year and always when the pub was quiet. Vickie said on these occasions she was not thinking about anything in particular, but simply concentrating on the job in hand. She has also experienced glasses moving forward in the bar and dropping down and heard the sound of footsteps from upstairs when Paul and Sue were out; she was informed by a former employee that they were supposed to be those of a young girl. She told me that knocking has been heard on the door leading to the stairs. On one occasion she was with barmaid Stacey and they both saw a light come on in a blown light bulb in the north-east corner of the pub.

Stacey Clare Hoare has worked there as a barmaid since about 2006 and has also witnessed glasses dropping from the bar, including one that moved half-way across the bar. She said the clock in the bar once fell down, which

*Staff at the Quay Inn. (l to r) Vickie Walters, Landlord Paul Brenson and Stacey Clare Hoare.*

could not be accounted for, and the television sometimes switches itself off. She, too, has heard the sound of footsteps running up and down upstairs, which she described as similar to those made by a child. According to Wareham resident Joy Leaton, a former landlady also heard the ghostly footsteps.

## An old property on the Quay

Vickie Walters described a frightening paranormal experience she had had in a property on the Quay when she stayed there one night with her friend Stacey Clare Hoare during Christmas 2010. Vickie described how at 4 a.m. she went cold and felt a presence on top of her. Stacey's dog started behaving wildly and barking (it later barked at the top of the stairs); interestingly, there was no reaction from the cat in the room. Stacey woke up and saw a black figure over Vickie and lots of silver face shapes around the room, which Stacey confirmed to me subsequently.

Vickie also said that paranormal activity was experienced in the top room of that house, which was always cold: Stacey's brother saw a woman in Victorian clothing, a bell was heard ringing in the room and lights used to dim.

Nicola Richards has lived at the property since July 2011 and has had a few experiences, but nothing very dramatic. Soon after moving in, she woke up one night and heard a voice saying, 'Mum, mum, mum', but admitted that it might have been a dream. She has felt someone touch her hand and also heard footsteps on the top floor, which is her daughter's bedroom.

## The Old Granary

Amy Steele is the General Manager of the Old Granary. The present building, which is more than 250 years old, serves as a restaurant and is attractively situated on the quay. Amy has lived and worked in the building since 2007 and has experienced some paranormal activity there herself.

There is a ghost, known as 'Cecil', who is thought to be of a man who hanged himself in a bedroom upstairs. Amy told me that she has regularly heard a sound at night like a squeaky gate, which is supposed to be of the metal chain that he used to hang himself. She and others have heard their names called in a loud whisper downstairs in the corridor near the bar and glasses have sometimes dropped off the shelf in the bar. Amy also mentioned a lady who worked there around the 1960s, reporting how she and her husband would hear footsteps in a room upstairs.

*Old Granary, Wareham*

Heather Sephton is just one member of staff who has had the experience of having her name called. She has worked there since 2010 and had not been told about the ghost; she described herself as fairly sceptical. One day in late April/early May 2012 Heather was standing behind the food bar when she heard someone shouting, 'Heather, Heather'. The time was about 2.30 p.m. and the Granary was nearly empty. Heather said she was in a relaxed state of mind when she heard her name called. Another member of staff also had a similar experience near the food bar around the same time of day as Heather when she heard her name called from the main restaurant in front of her; initially, she thought it was the Assistant Manager, but then realised it was not. It was lunch time and the Granary was very busy. She also had the feeling on occasions that someone was watching her from near the door when she was in the washroom.

Speaking in October 2012, Ben Holden told me that he had been working at the Granary for about a month. On the second or third day he was in the top restaurant when he heard a voice coming from the wash-up area calling his name; he described the voice as high-pitched and male. The name calling occurred to him on another occasion when he was in the top restaurant: that time the voice came from behind him and near the toilet area. It was only later that he learned that other staff had also had the experience of their names being called.

Another member of staff, who has worked there for several years, told me that he too has heard his name called on several occasions; he described it as sounding like the voice of a colleague but not quite the same. He also showed me the area behind the bar where a glass had fallen down, but the strange thing was that it had moved back by several feet rather than dropping straight down.

## The Grey Lady at the Priory

The Priory, which has been run as a hotel by the Turner family since 1976, is located in a peaceful setting between Lady St Mary's Church and the River Frome and contains more than 4 acres of beautiful gardens. The house dates from the early 16th century and incorporates stones that were taken from the ruins of older buildings on the site. Saint Aldhelm, who was Bishop of Sherborne, is known to have visited the area in 700 and to have founded a religious house, which was probably on the same site, and a convent of nuns was recorded at Wareham by Bishop Asser in 876. Skeletons found just outside the Priory's walls are believed to be the remains of some of those nuns. During the 11th century the nuns were replaced by Benedictine monks and 250 years later the religious house was transferred to the Carthusians until the time of Henry VIII's Dissolution of the Monasteries in 1536.

John Turner's stepson, Jeremy Merchant, now runs the Priory. He has not personally experienced any paranormal phenomena, but told me in May 2012 that the figure of a grey lady, thought to be that of a nun, has been reported occasionally. Jeremy described three significant sightings of the grey lady, which have occurred over a number of years. One concerned a couple that come to stay at the Priory from time to time: on this occasion it was Christmas, sometime in the early 2000s, and the couple were staying in Room 7 (known as Brownsea Room). The man saw a figure, whom he described as a lady in a grey tunic, in the hallway; his wife did not see her. A second sighting occurred to a female member of staff, who was opening

*The Priory Hotel, Wareham*

up during the winter time: she turned on the lights and saw the same figure in the foyer. The third occasion was in the summer when a mother and daughter were sitting on the lawn outside. The daughter said to her mother, 'Did you see the lady?' Her mother had not seen anything, but the daughter maintained that a lady kept coming out of the doorway by the Yew tree. When I returned to the Priory in late June 2012, Jeremy told me that his sister had seen the ghost of the grey lady in Room 7 within the previous month while staying in the room on a visit: she had woken up suddenly in the night to find a woman's figure standing over the bed and looking down on her.

Swanage residents Peter and Vikki Fooks stayed at the Priory over the weekend of 3/4 February 2012 as Peter's treat to celebrate a special anniversary. They were given a large bedroom, located above the dining room, and duly retired on the first night of their stay. Peter described waking up in the middle of the night and seeing a lady standing to his left next to the bed and looking down at him while Vikki was asleep to his right. His immediate reaction was one of shock, thinking that they had overslept and that the lady was a waitress or maid. The lady, who was tall and around 60 years old, was wearing a black dress with white trimmings. To Peter's consternation, the figure quickly vanished. It is probable that this figure is the same as that reported by the other witnesses. Peter did not see the lady on the second night they stayed in the room.

## The Former Flower Shop in South Street

Jillian Emery lived in Wareham for three and a half years and owned what used to be the flower shop opposite the Black Bear (she still owns the building). She said that she would sometimes get the feeling in the shop that someone was standing behind her, and the previous owner had reported a very cold feeling in the middle room of the building. Jillian also described feeling a presence in the lane between the Quay and Lady St Mary's Church and once had the sensation of some presence following her in Pound Lane.

## St John's Hill

St John's Hill is a very old part of Wareham and it is believed that two royal mints may have been in this area during the reign of King Athelstan in the 10th century. Human remains dating back 600 years were found recently. I have collected three stories from this area that relate to three different properties.

The first account was sent to me by Joy Leaton, who lived at her parents' house (dating to about 1800) in St John's Hill until 1989:

'I was in the sitting room downstairs chatting with my boyfriend. It was about 10 or 11 o'clock at night. The television was switched off and the kitchen door was open, but the kitchen light was off. My dog was lying on the floor facing the kitchen. He started to whimper and his head was raised and his ears were back. I spoke to him to calm him, but it didn't work. I stood up and leaned forward to take a look at what was upsetting him, expecting to see that the cat had brought in a mouse or something, but instead I saw a very clear shadow of a man in a cavalier style hat. It simply passed along the kitchen wall and disappeared in just a second or two. The figure did not seem to be aware of my presence at all. It was a fleeting but very clear image. I was surprised, but didn't feel at all threatened or afraid.'

Joy's mother, Marion Taylor, has lived in the house since 1964 and told me that a sister of Joy also saw the shadow of the cavalier, but on that occasion it was in a bedroom upstairs. Marion has had several experiences there herself: one night she woke up with the distinct impression that someone was in the room, but when she turned on the light she could not see anything. Not long after her husband had died, one of the light bulbs kept flashing on and off. She said, 'If that's you, stop it', whereupon the flashing ceased.

Marion Taylor also described how a couple and a friend all stayed in a property in St John's Hill for 7–8 weeks in early 2012. One of them reported regularly hearing a voice in the night saying, 'It's George'. Marion said that it is not known whether anyone of that name was ever associated with the house.

The third account relates to a young lady referred to here as 'Kate', who reported some paranormal activity at a cottage in St John's Hill in 2009. Her mother rented the cottage (using one bedroom) for about 6 months and Kate herself stayed there for about 6 weeks. The second bedroom was kept locked by the owner, who stored some of her belongings there, and both Kate and her mother had uneasy feelings about that room. One evening her mother went up to her room to prepare for bed and, on returning from the bathroom, found that the curtains in her bedroom had been drawn across, but with a gap left between; she herself never left a gap whenever she drew the curtains. She called down to Kate to ask if she had touched them, but she had not. Two or three weeks later Kate went into the dining room, which she was using as a bedroom, and discovered that the duvet covers had been drawn back as if ready for her to go to bed. She could not explain this as there was no one else there.

# The Black Bear Hotel

The Black Bear Hotel is located in South Street and is a famous landmark in the town, with its unusual effigy of a black bear prominently positioned above the porch, where travellers would have waited for the stage coach. The hotel dates from after 1762, as an earlier building on the site was destroyed in the fire of that year. There is apparently a local legend that if the bear falls from the porch roof, the world will end!

*Black Bear Hotel, Wareham*

Recent paranormal activity has been recorded in several places in the Black Bear Hotel. A former landlady told me in January 2012 how she had seen the figure of a man at the bar on several occasions. She described him as slim, in his early 30s and wearing a long black coat and hat; when he appeared, which was always in the evenings, he would stand near the bar door and dishwasher. His clothes suggested he would date to around the beginning of the last century. Another phenomenon she witnessed was a mauve light, which sometimes came across the bar, usually in the evening.

Former barman Jamie Trafford told me that a friend of his had been pushed in the back in the corridor between the bar and toilets about a week prior to my visit. Another barman apparently saw the figure of a little girl in the corridor in 2010 and footsteps have been heard there. A psychic who visited the Black Bear claimed that a little girl was buried beneath the floor in the toilet.

The paranormal activity is not confined to the ground floor. The figure of an old lady has been seen upstairs in Room 16 by several visitors and cold feelings experienced there. A former landlady saw orbs in Room 11 and heard footsteps upstairs when there was no one present.

## The Conservative Club

Wareham Conservative Club, located in South Street, is set back a little from the road and was originally built in 1830 as a Unitarian Chapel. The Palladian-style building was used for church meetings until the 1960s when it was converted into the Conservative Club.

According to locals, the building has a reputation for being haunted and a previous landlady, who lived upstairs, experienced the television switching itself on. The barman, Dwain Musselwhite, lives in the flat above and described two strange incidents that had happened in August 2012. One occurred at night when he heard the alarm going off and then the television coming on at full blast, which happened twice, and was reminiscent of the landlady's experience; he could not account for it as no one else was in the building at the time. The other happened one morning about 9 a.m. when he came down to the bar to do some work: he noticed a chair in the centre of the room a few feet away from one of the tables, so he pushed it back. Dwain carried on working, but then, about 20 minutes later, he found that the chair was back out again. This was very disconcerting as there was

*Conservative Club, Wareham*

nobody in the building apart from himself. Another strange experience, also in the morning when he was alone, took place a few weeks later after he had shut the fire door to the bar and heard it click to: he was walking away when he heard another click, turned round and, to his amazement, watched the door open by itself.

## The Red Lion

The Red Lion Hotel is located in the centre of Wareham near the junction of West Street and North Street. It was originally a posting inn, which was established in the late 1600s, and in 1859 was described as being a commercial inn, posting house, market house and an Inland Revenue office. In the late 19th century the Red Lion was Wareham's main hotel and was run by Cornelius Yearsley, who was also the town's mayor. Lisa and Lee Sainsbury have been running the Red Lion since January 2011 and have undertaken an extensive refurbishment.

Tina Hills used to work as a chambermaid at the hotel and described how she saw a ghost in one of the cellars. This cellar, where linen is kept, is separate from the main building and has a noticeably low ceiling; it is close to where the stables would have been. The sighting occurred around 10.30 a.m. in late March 2012 when she had gone there to sort out some linen, as part of her routine. Tina was bent over, absorbed in her work, when she noticed a pair of light-coloured buckled shoes. She then saw that a man's figure clad in a black cape and white socks/stockings was standing

*Red Lion, Wareham*

there, just as a coachman of several hundred years ago might have appeared. Tina wasted no time in getting out of the cellar as quickly as possible. She described it as her first ever experience of a ghost and is pleased that she can now say that they exist; she hopes she may see the figure again.

A former barmaid apparently had a strange experience in 2012 in another cellar near the bar. She had gone down there early one morning and then heard footsteps and seen a shadow go past the door leading to the cellar. When she went back up, she asked if anyone had gone past the cellar and was told that no one had.

Vickie Walters, who works at the Quay Inn, used to work at the Red Lion in about 2007. She said that she would sometimes feel that something was watching her in Rooms 7, 8 and 9 and that on occasions, when sitting alone in the bar, she had the feeling that someone was walking past.

Lisa Sainsbury said that in Victorian times there was reputedly a haunted cupboard where a severed hand had been seen. Lisa has not experienced anything herself so far at the Red Lion, but used to run the Brunswick at Charminster, Bournemouth, where several paranormal incidents occurred.

## A doppelganger encounter

A resident from Wareham had the disconcerting experience of seeing his double and at the time seemed to be in that state between wakefulness and sleep, sometimes referred to as the hypnagogic state, where paranormal activity has a tendency to occur. He is fairly sceptical himself, but has agreed to his wife sending me the following account:

'It was before the boys were born and we were in bed asleep, having a lie-in at the weekend. My husband became aware that our dog (who was in a kennel and pen in the back garden) was barking, the kind of bark that attracts your attention. He said that he was thinking that he really ought to wake up and go and investigate what was going on outside. When he eventually did rouse himself to actually get up, he said that he stood up and, as he did so, he saw himself heading back to bed. He said that his 'other self' walked through him and, as he did so, he felt a shudder go right through his body.'

## Anglebury House Hotel

There is a distinct feeling of stepping back in time when one enters the Anglebury House Hotel, so it is perhaps not surprising to find some interesting paranormal phenomena recorded there in recent years. Situated in North Street, parts of the building date back to the 16th century and survived the disastrous fire that destroyed much of the old town in 1762. Much of the interior is early 18th century, including the front part adjoining the street, where one can look through the windows, admiring the quaint décor and fireplaces. Both Thomas Hardy and T.E. Lawrence (of Arabia) spent time drinking coffee here and the latter also lived in the building for a while (Lawrence's ghost has reportedly been seen on the South Bridge at Wareham).

In November 2011 Amanda Robins described an experience she had had late one summer evening about 15 years previously when she was walking past the Anglebury and happened to glance through the window. She saw, to her amazement, two people clad in 17th century attire, one on either side of the fireplace in the main restaurant: on one side stood a man dressed as a musketeer, wearing a hat with a feather in it and a sword by his side; on the other was a woman in a long-sleeved black dress with a white pinafore over it, such as a servant might have worn. Amanda briefly glanced away and on looking back found the two figures had vanished. She also told me that she had had a friend who had worked in the tea room at that time, who reported scones lifting themselves off from the counter and falling onto the floor.

Having had my interest aroused by Amanda's account, I contacted the owner of the hotel, Jane Spencer, and then paid a visit in early December 2011. Jane told me that she had been running it for the past 12 years and that a number of people had reported paranormal experiences, especially prior to 2006, when the building was revamped.

*Anglebury House Hotel, Wareham*

Jane has experienced several weird phenomena herself. The most bizarre was when she was in the kitchen with the chef, Carol; as Carol opened the fridge door, a small milk container fell out and tumbled onto the floor. That in itself would not have been unusual, but what happened next was: the spilt milk followed the container as if in slow motion and then went back inside, with both Jane and Carol watching in amazement. Another strange incident occurred overnight in the restaurant around 2002/3 when a painting that had been hanging near the window was found lying on the table the next morning; as Jane explained, the room had been locked, so no resident could have gone in to take down the picture. Then there was the occasion when a wake was held at the Anglebury late one evening. Someone suggested that a drink should be bought for the deceased, with another person replying, 'It's no good, he can't drink it'. At that moment a bottle of gin fell onto the floor and smashed. Jane witnessed this and was annoyed that the gin had been wasted. Coincidence? Who knows!

Jane's son, Andrew Welch, also works at the Anglebury and he showed me the staircase where he has felt the presence of a little girl from time to time. He described her as having curly hair and wearing a long dress, and he has sensed her sitting at the bottom of the stairs, just as he has come down and passed the lower steps, which has sent a shiver down his spine. A few visitors, too, have sensed the young girl's presence, as well as the smell of oil lamps, which would have been used in the past. There have also been several sightings of young people in rooms upstairs: someone called Maggie reported seeing small children in Room 2, with the sighting thought to have been around 2004. Even more remarkable was the comment by the Ofsted inspector who spent a night in Room 3 in the early 2000s and said, according to Jane, the next morning: 'It was unfair to have put me in a room with an 18-year-old girl I could not touch: I think she must have hanged herself'. Rooms 2 and 3, it should be noted, were originally joined.

## The King's Arms

The King's Arms in North Street at one time was a coach house and stables. The pub is more than 100 years old and the building over 500.

Jane Spencer ran the King's Arms from November 2003 to May 2006 and said that they always felt that there was something in the cellar. On one occasion the alarm went off in the night and, on coming down, she found some mushroom trays right in front of the flat door. The strange thing about this was that the trays could only have been put there from the kitchen side as it would not have been possible to have first put something there and then shut the flat door and the building had been locked.

Barman Brian Horsey, speaking in December 2011, said that the landlady's partner, Ralph, has experienced a few things, though the landlady herself is sceptical. One incident occurred in about 2009 when Ralph put a tool-box over two barrels in the cellar; after about half an hour the tool-box started to tilt. Another occasion was a year later when a glass and the drip tray on which it was resting both suddenly fell on the floor; as the drip tray is firmly fixed, this is difficult to explain.

## Farwells

Lesley and Mark Howlett run Farwells newsagents in North Street and have lived in the flat since the mid-1990s. Part of the building dates back to the 1700s. Lesley described several paranormal experiences that had occurred in the flat above. She recalled the occasion around 2005 when Mark was in the kitchen with her father doing some renovation. Mark turned round and saw a young girl apparently looking at what they were doing. No one else was in the building at the time. Around the same time, Lesley herself had the experience, while in the bath, of seeing a shadow go past towards the bedroom and disappear; as there are no windows in the passageway, she could not explain it. She said she has sometimes had the sensation of being watched, but has never felt frightened. One other strange incident occurred in the late 1990s when her name badge, which she used when working at a local school, disappeared from its usual place in the kitchen, only to mysteriously reappear about a month later in the same location.

## A house in North Street

The following account was sent to me by Hugh Elmes and refers to a house in North Street, where he lived for many years; his father had moved there prior to 1940. The building next door was apparently a pub in the 19th century.

'I lived in North Street as a child. I stayed on after my parents had left the house so lived there for approximately 36 years. My father said that when they first moved into the property, one night he was sitting down reading the newspaper and the light in the centre of the dining room started to sway backwards and forwards. All the doors and windows were closed at that time, so it couldn't have been caused by a draught. Father could not understand it and thought the best thing he could do was go on to bed. Next day he fitted a flush-mounted lamp to the ceiling and never had any more trouble. As kids we used to hear people walking along our passage, but when we looked there was no one there (note that all the family and also visitors heard the footsteps). We learnt to live with this, but if we had company it would cause quite a lot of interest! We used to call them Gilby the ghost and friends.

I left the house in 1964 and returned again in 1967. By this time I was married. The noises still carried on but soon my wife got used to them as well, after all they did us no harm. We had purchased a parrot and a cat. Some evenings as we sat there, we could hear the noise of people entering the property and the cat and the parrot would look at the door waiting for someone to enter. Sometimes the cat's fur would rise, but still no one was there.

We had a Welsh dresser with plates on display. One night my wife and I sat there with the cat and parrot when suddenly we saw a plate fall in slow motion from the top shelf of the dresser. It bounced off the work surface of the dresser and spun (slowly) as it landed on the ground. The plate did not break and we put it back on the dresser and never had any more problems. We still heard the noises but there was no set pattern. As a matter of interest, I still have the Welsh dresser and plates.'

## Hyde House – the girl in the fireplace

The young lady referred to as 'Kate' in the third account from St John's Hill also had an experience at the age of 10 when she was staying at Hyde House near Wareham on a school trip. She was sharing a room with several girls, one of whom had been unwell during that day, and Kate recalled lying awake in the middle of the night and suddenly seeing the figure of a girl (also aged about 10) in a pale nightgown climb out of the old fireplace in the room and step onto a suitcase at the head of the sick girl's bed. Kate distinctly remembers that the suitcase did not sag in any way, just as if the girl had no weight. The girl then kissed the sick girl on the forehead and Kate asked who she was and what she was doing out of bed, promising not to tell. The girl immediately vanished and Kate screamed loudly and woke up the rest of the house. The teachers tried to reassure her that she had just been dreaming, but Kate knew what she had seen and was too frightened to return to the room that night.

## Chapter 3

# The Royal Oak, Swanage – a Very Haunted Location

The Royal Oak, situated at the western end of the High Street in Herston, Swanage, presents a traditional stone facade in keeping with the local quarry working of the area, but rather like Dr Who's Tardis gives a distinct impression of being bigger on the inside when you pass through the door. Rachael Aplin, who is now the owner, has been running the pub since 2005, but also worked there in the mid-1980s. The building has been used as a pub for many years and is first listed as a beer shop in 1834 when it was run by a Mr Lockyer. In 1848 Thomas and Syndonia Stevens took over the building and ran it as a pub for 30 years; the name

*Royal Oak, north side*

'Royal Oak' first appears in a trade directory for 1857. It is clear from the narrow staircases and low ceilings that the building is much older than 1834 and it is believed it was originally four cottages, with the two oldest being at the rear and possibly dating to the early 18th century, or perhaps even earlier. The Tudor Subsidy Rolls of 1525 and 1544 list 15 and 18 people respectively as living at Herston and eligible to pay tax; the name 'Herston' is mentioned in the Domesday Book and Romano-British graves have been found in the vicinity, so it can be seen that the local area has quite a history.

At ground level the Royal Oak today consists of the bar, dining room, kitchen, pool room and cellar, with toilets situated to the rear of the kitchen. There are three bedrooms, a living room, kitchen and bathroom on the second floor and in this kitchen there is a cupboard which in the past was connected to the bar below by means of a staircase. The top storey has three bedrooms and a store room. The pub garden, which has a southerly aspect, was the location of a grisly find around 2000 when the neck vertebra of a woman was unearthed and dated to at least 300 years ago, after being sent away for analysis.

The Royal Oak has seen considerable paranormal activity in recent years and appears to be the most haunted location in Purbeck. There has been a variety of phenomena witnessed, including multiple sightings of ghosts, inexplicable noises and smells, pictures coming off the walls, the sensation of being touched, strange incidents concerning glasses and curtains, and displacements in time. The pub has also acted as a magnet for mediums and spiritualists, but it is important to note that a broad spectrum of people have experienced the phenomena, including a number of sceptics. During the course of my investigations I interviewed nearly 40 witnesses, most of whom are local, come from different backgrounds and represent a wide age range. I also found it interesting that at least as many men as women have had paranormal experiences in the pub. Many of these people are regular customers, or have worked there. It is also only fair to point out that there are other regular customers who do not seem to experience any paranormal phenomena in the pub. It would seem that paranormal activity was occurring at the Royal Oak as far back as 1998 and probably earlier, as the following accounts bear witness.

# Earlier Paranormal Experiences

## Jsanine Jenkin

Some of the earlier phenomena were witnessed by Jsanine Jenkin, who lived at the pub for about 16 months from early 1998 when her mother Christine was running it. When I interviewed Jsanine in November 2011, she told me that the first paranormal incident occurred about a couple of months after they had moved in. Christine was behind the bar and Jsanine was on the other side when she witnessed an empty Guinness pint glass ascend from the counter, go over the Coke stand and then drop on the floor behind the bar, where it smashed. The next incident was in June 1998 when her young son Christopher was asleep by the bed in Jsanine's room upstairs when suddenly their cat began growling and jumped onto Jsanine before lying down beside Christopher. She then heard the sound of loud footsteps on the landing, as if made by a workman in heavy boots. The noise woke up her mother, who was asleep in the bedroom on the other side of the landing, and Jsanine recalled seeing her peeping through the doorway to see what was going on. She estimated that the sound of the footsteps lasted 3–4 minutes. Something similar occurred, just 2 months later: Christine's friend Sue was staying and they both heard the sound of someone running upstairs when there was no one else in the pub, with the noise lasting a few minutes. They initially thought that a burglar had broken in and were on the point of calling the police. Jsanine remembers a previous landlord asking whether they had heard the landing walker, which indicates that paranormal activity was occurring prior to 1998.

Another strange occurrence concerned Jsanine's son, Christopher, when he was 4 years old. Jsanine described watching him sitting on the wall by the terraced area in the garden and apparently having a conversation with an invisible entity; this conversation even included answering questions, suggesting that some kind of dialogue was taking place. When she asked Christopher who he had been talking to, he replied simply, 'Him'. A woman later reported that Christopher had started to use the word 'twin' when playing with her own son. Christopher had, in fact, had a twin who had died, but Jsanine said that he had not been aware of the word 'twin' before his strange conversation.

Jsanine mentioned several people who had found the pub scary. There was one couple who were staying upstairs, where the woman was afraid to be left on her own. Another instance concerned a workman who had been sitting in the bar and insisted he had spoken to Christine when she had, in fact, not been present; he was so frightened by this experience that he left the pub and slept outside in his van. Jsanine said that she often got the feeling of being watched when she was cleaning, particularly outside the ladies. She also reported an unpleasant sensation in the kitchen.

## Mark Elford

In September 2011 Mark Elford related several incredible experiences that had happened to him at the Royal Oak and described the pub as having 'a trapped emotion which cannot pass' (emotion waiting for freedom), saying that 'the key to emotional things can be unlocked here'. His first experience occurred about 8–10 years previously, soon after a fridge had been moved (disturbance to a building may sometimes trigger paranormal activity) when he saw a lady behind the bar in the right-hand corner; she was dressed in a gown and an old-fashioned cap, such as a Victorian lady might have worn. Mark saw the lady again more recently and said that she appeared to be in her 40s but looked older (as people in the past often did); her gown was made of rags or pieces of different material stitched together. The lady had a lost expression about her and Mark followed her through to the pool room near the cellar, where he saw her raise her hands and point to the ground. He sensed intuitively her name was Edith (nickname 'Edie') and that she was waiting for her husband, who worked in the stone industry, to return from abroad with some Canadian pink stone, perhaps for a headstone. The woman had had a child with another man, but it had died. Mark felt that her husband had returned too late, only to find that Edith had died, and he stressed the strong emotional feeling he received from the triangle of the man, woman and child and also the pink stone.

Mark's first sighting of 'Edith' seemed to lead to a chain of events and he felt that perhaps some kind of channel opened up as a result of his acknowledgement of her. On one occasion, for instance, he had a sudden impulse to speak to a woman in the bar concerning some jewellery, which not only proved accurate but also very beneficial to her. Mark has had an unpleasant impression in the west bedroom and thinks that a woman may have been raped there; he also felt that the roof that can now be seen from the south window was not there.

Another remarkable experience occurred on a Tuesday night in about 2007 when a pool game was being played and the white ball came off the table in the direction of the door on the south-west side near the cellar. Mark went over to pick up the ball and then had the amazing sensation of being outside, with the feeling of air on him, even though he was still inside. He described being behind a wall with steps going up into the garden where there was a wall with pink stones. He seemed to be in a backyard where washing would have been done. The whole experience he described as being like in another dimension, or a displacement of time. He also appeared to be invisible and he could not see anything material related to his body (his consciousness was normal). Mark has no recollection of picking up the white ball, but somehow got back into the pool room in his body and normal time frame, but he said he has often wondered what would have happened if he had walked down the garden. 'Would I still be here?' he asked. While we were talking, he mentioned the year 1710, but was not clear why he had said it. Later, we examined the area around the door where he had had his experience and also went out into the garden and he explained that in his vision the level would have been several feet higher and that the garden was flatter than now with an allotment.

# More Recent Happenings

## Rachael Aplin and Andrew Power

When I first spoke to Rachael Aplin in April 2011, she told me how she had never really wanted to run the Royal Oak and had an aversion to it; she had hoped to manage another pub in Swanage. However, a friend of hers, Terri Powell, who is a local medium, insisted that she would eventually buy the Royal Oak and described to me how they had been walking in the nearby fields one day and the insight had come to her. This was to come true as Rachael became not only the landlady but also later the owner. Rachael said that she feels she has lived in the pub before and has the sensation of wearing a long dress, which is something she does not normally wear. Under hypnotic regression, Rachael gave the name of 'Sid', which might possibly refer to Syndonia, the wife of the former landlord, Thomas Stevens. The name Syndonia struck me as very unusual (it comes from Sidon in the Middle East) and, after doing a little research, I was amazed to discover that Syndonia's parents had been the great great grandparents of local historian Reg Saville, who had sent me a ghost story concerning them only a couple of weeks earlier and had himself suggested that I contact Rachael about the paranormal activity at the pub after she had asked him to do some historical research. 'Syndonia' seemed to be a kind of synchronicity that had brought the three of us together. Further research led to the discovery that Syndonia and some of her family are buried at Northbrook Cemetery, Swanage. Her daughter Elizabeth died in July 1859 at the age of 7 as a result of a wasting disease related to tuberculosis and it is possible that one of the ghosts in the pub may be that of her.

*Rachael Aplin in the Royal Oak Garden*

Some of the current paranormal activity seems to date from 2008 when a friend of Rachael's died and some of his ashes were placed in the pub garden. Then, on 5 August 2009 a stranger, who subsequently told Rachael his name was Andrew Power, called at the pub with a friend in the late evening and asked to be served, though Rachael was keen to close as she was not feeling well. Rachael was talking with a friend about her friend's husband's suicide when Andrew suddenly felt the man's presence and described him to them. He went on to describe Rachael's late grandfather, apparently very accurately, and also a friend of Rachael's who had died; Andrew felt that these very people were standing there at the end of the bar. He and Rachael then had a long conversation about paranormal phenomena at the pub and eventually Andrew asked if he could see the haunted room upstairs, which had been mentioned in the course of their discussion. (Note that this was the east bedroom on the second floor, but much of the paranormal activity later transferred itself to the west bedroom on the third storey.) Rachael was reluctant to allow him to do this, but after much persuasion told him to go and find the room for himself. Andrew then takes up the story:

'We went to the bottom of the stairs and Rachael let me go upstairs first; there was a funny sensation on the stairs, but instinctively I knew where to go. I carried on through the lounge into the next-door room where a horrible feeling took over me. I felt it very hard to go any further into the room and felt very sick. I could feel the hairs stand up on the back of my neck; she was quite disturbed by it all. We went back into the lounge and I really didn't feel any better; I just wanted to get out of there. I continued to look around the rest of the upstairs and told Rachael to change her bedroom as she shouldn't be in there. We went back downstairs and sat and talked for what seemed like forever; I described the lady upstairs as beautiful, long dark hair, quite short, but when she opened her mouth the most hideous teeth were shown to me (I was not expecting that!). I thought her name may be Bernadette and she had been very badly treated there.'

(It is of great interest that prior to Andrew's experience, medium Terri had picked up the image in the pub of an attractive woman with long, straight black hair, who had some of her teeth missing.)

Andrew Power predicted that one day he would come to live in the pub and work there. Subsequently, he came to the Royal Oak to do a lot of dry-stone walling in the garden. He tried staying in the pub for a short time, but found it very difficult to sleep and always woke up feeling completely drained. He described what happened on one of the first nights he slept there:

'I woke up sensing a man sat in a chair in the middle of the room (this was the west room on the third floor) who was very unhappy with what was going on there; I didn't know what it was about. I was a little disturbed when I found out from Rachael that I had described a previous landlord who had lived there some years earlier. This was also confirmed to me when the next day I met his son when I was out with Rachael and was very shocked at the resemblance he bore to his father.'

The former landlord that Andrew had seen in the west room was Eddie Taylor. It was also from this room that Andrew had a vision of an orchard in the garden. There is no doubt in Andrew's mind that the Royal Oak is haunted.

# Female Apparitions

There have been multiple sightings of a number of apparitions in the last few years, with a host of witnesses. At least one young girl appears to be haunting the pub and various people have reported seeing apparitions of young women. Mark Knight, speaking to me in June 2011, described how, about a year previously, he had been working in the bar and standing by the hatchway when he heard a noise coming from the kitchen, though the lights were off there. He felt the hairs on the back of his neck stand on end as he saw the kitchen door swing open and a young girl's head and hand appear. He described the girl as having medium-length blonde hair. The same ghost may have been seen by regular customer Melanie Dyke (though she could not tell if the figure were male or female), who reported an experience she had once had in the bar when she glimpsed a figure on the other side of the kitchen door, walking from side to side; there was no one in the kitchen at the time. Martin Egan, who used to stay in the pub, saw a number of ghosts, including a young girl between the sitting room on the second floor and the staircase; he said she was aged about 9 or 10, had long, light-brown hair and was wearing a white frilly dress with a zip at the back. Rachael's father, Raymond, told me that he had seen the figure of a girl going up the stairs, whom he described as aged between 6 and 10 and wearing a summer dress. In March 2011 photographer Trevor Rich also had an experience on the stairs and described it in these words:

'I had finished shooting a party in the pub when I went upstairs to get my camera bag. Despite not having any belief whatsoever in the paranormal, I always feel apprehensive about going upstairs. I was fairly lubricated from a night on the local ales and as I picked up my camera and turned to descend the staircase, I saw a young girl walking along the corridor beside me (parallel to the stairs). She was wearing a white nightgown and a white bonnet. From what hair I could see, it was dark, but it was tied up under the bonnet. I didn't feel any fear. I simply looked away and left.'

Trevor attributes his experience to his inebriated state and the expectation of seeing something rather than a real ghost, but it needs, perhaps, to be put into the context of all the other sightings.

Another interesting sighting of a girl occurred one afternoon in February 2012 when I was discussing my book with Rachael and Jan Poole, a regular customer, in the bar. Lukasz Domagala, who stayed in the pub from Christmas 2011, came in and Rachael asked him to go upstairs for something. He reappeared a few minutes later and, on listening to our conversation about sightings of the young girl, said, 'Actually, I think I may have just seen her!' Jan and I then went upstairs with Lukasz, so he could show us what had happened. He explained how he had opened the living room door and caught a glimpse of a girl's face beyond the next door which was ajar. He then walked into the next room and saw the girl again behind another door that was open, just as if she were playing a game. He described her as aged between 10 and 15, having long, wavy black hair and wearing a long grey-white dress or smock. Lucasz's description was reminiscent of a girl that I had myself seen sitting in the dining room at the Halloween party in 2011 and who had later mysteriously disappeared, but as there were a lot of people present, she could have just slipped away unnoticed.

There have been other sightings of a girl or woman in the bar area. Both Rachael and a former barmaid saw a female figure behind the counter walking towards the fridge and then disappearing round the corner. In April 2011 Kath Payne described how she had seen a young girl in the same area disappear into the wall. At the time she was sitting in the bar with a group of friends, having a conversation, when she felt something drawing her attention to look in that direction: after glancing that way several times, she suddenly saw the figure and the other people present said that Kath had a look of amazement on her face. A former landlady confirmed to Rachael that she had once seen a girl disappear through the wall in the bar where the crisp packets hang. It is also possible that Jan Poole may have caught sight of a female figure at the bar in the autumn of 2010: she was sitting on a stool at the bar and could see what appeared to be someone bending low on the floor on the other side of the bar. She caught glimpses of flashes of blue and thought that it was barmaid Lil Hosegood sorting out glasses, but could not hear any sound. After a few minutes, she leaned over to have a proper look and realised to her amazement that no one was there. Lil herself said she had once seen from the bar counter the figure of a young woman, or child, in a dark coat walking along the corridor; no one else had witnessed this as they were not looking in that direction. Rachael's daughter, Bryony, and Rachael's mother, Gill, both saw simultaneously the figure of what may have been a child going through the bar towards the pool room; Bryony said the figure was wearing a coat and she also told me that shortly before this, a cigar had fallen off the shelf in the bar, closely followed by

*Royal Oak Bar*

a box of matches. From the above accounts, there may be several young girls/women involved and it is known from census records that a number of young women lived in the pub at various times, including, of course, Elizabeth Stevens, who died there in 1859.

Ghosts of the fairer sex at the Royal Oak are by no means confined to the very young. Customer Brian Winters, speaking to me in October 2011, described a remarkable experience he had had about 2 years previously. He was standing near the north-west corner of the bar by the fire and was about to walk across the room. Two chairs had been placed by the fire as the weather was cold and Brian noticed a young lady in her late 20s sitting in one of the chairs by the bar counter. As he walked across, he said, 'Excuse me, I'll have to move the chair', but on looking back, there was no one there. The young woman had completely vanished. Barmaid Kate Brown twice saw the figure of a little old lady in the garden in the late evening during the autumn of 2012. On both occasions (6 weeks apart) Kate had gone out of the back door into the garden when her attention was drawn to the lady, who was clad in a white dress and white bonnet, walking from the shelter and crossing the path to the lawn. Medium Terri has picked up on a number of female ghosts/spirits at the pub. The one she is aware of more than any is a large lady called Annie, but she has also seen an old lady in a rocking chair in the west room as well as a girl Lizzie (Elizabeth Stevens?) whom she thinks died there, and a woman with a baby in the east bedroom.

# Male Apparitions

Male apparitions have also been seen at the Royal Oak by a number of witnesses. Nick and Gina Bathe have been coming to stay at the pub for several years. Gina told me how she has twice seen the figure of a quarryman. The first time he was sitting in the corner of the pool room and she described the experience as being like something out of a black and white film. Gina saw him again in August 2011: on that occasion she was coming from the ladies into the pool room and she experienced a vision in which the west side of the pool room had changed into a bar and she could see the quarryman leaning on the corner of the bar counter (Rachael confirmed that there used to be a bar in that area). On both occasions the quarryman was similarly dressed and Gina described him as a slender man of about 60 dating from the late 19th century, with grey hair and a rather wrinkled face. In appearance he was a smart-looking, working man wearing a white shirt with the sleeves rolled up; he wore a handkerchief around his neck and his trousers were hitched up, with a belt lower down. Mediums Terri Powell and Angie Harrison-Page have also reported seeing the figure of a quarryman.

A similar though younger figure was seen by Kath Payne in the garden on the evening of 8 December 2011. Kath was sitting on the step having a cigarette when a man's figure appeared by the shed close to her. She described him as being in his 40s and wearing a very loose, white, long-sleeved, baggy shirt, or smock, with no collar; he had braces over this garment and was also wearing a pair of light-coloured long trousers. As he stood by the shed door, he lit something, either a cigarette or pipe, and then walked forward a few yards, all the time moving his arms to adjust his braces, before vanishing at the bottom of the path by the stones. Kath said that she had had no feeling that it was a ghost before the figure disappeared and described her state of mind at the time as being very relaxed. The man may date back to the early 20th century from his appearance. It is possible that the shed might have been used as an outdoor toilet in the past; the noticeable adjusting of the braces suggests that the man may have just pulled up his trousers.

Jsanine Jenkin also had an outdoor sighting in 2010 when she was sitting on the front wall outside the pub at about 5 p.m. Her attention was drawn to a little old man walking along the pavement from the direction of nearby Days Road; she watched him stop by the gap in the low wall between the pub and the adjoining cottage on the west side and then walk into the north wall of the pub and disappear. She was so disconcerted by what she had seen that she knocked on the cottage next door to check that the man had not gone in there, only to be greeted by a different man opening the door. Jsanine described the old man as being short, well-dressed and apparently bald, but wearing a cap on his head; she put him at about 80. It is important to note that a door used to exist where the old man had disappeared. Interestingly, Martin Egan told me that on the morning of 24 June 2011 at about 10 a.m., he was painting the ceiling in the bar when he saw a couple in old-fashioned clothes walk from near the west side of the bar and disappear into the north wall, which is roughly where that door would have been, so it would seem that ghosts can go through from both sides. Martin also told me that the second night he had stayed at the pub in 2009 he saw a grey, elderly man sitting in the north-west corner of the bar; he was wearing tiny glasses and a waistcoat and Martin said that he looked to be in his late 80s and probably dated from the 19th century. Rachael and Nick and Gina Bathe were aware of a presence in that corner early one morning in May 2011 on account of creaking noises coming from the seat, just as if someone were sitting there. Rachael asked if anyone was present and this was shortly followed by a loud noise at the bar; it was then discovered that the drinks hose had detached itself and fallen, though this would have been almost impossible to have occurred on its own.

Perhaps one of the most remarkable ghostly sightings of all was through a computer video link in Poland. Lukasz Domagala was given the west bedroom when he arrived at the Royal Oak and soon afterwards he started to get the feeling that someone was watching him from the side of the room near the window as he came upstairs and opened the door; the feeling was strong enough to make the hairs on his neck stand on end. Then, on 11 January 2012 he was lying on the bed facing away from the window with his computer open and having a conversation with his wife in Poland. His wife could see him on the bed through the computer video link and suddenly said, 'Who's with you?' She had seen the figure of a man behind him putting on a black coat and walking towards the door. This must rank as one of the most long-distance sightings of a ghost! Lucasz also found that his sleep pattern had changed and he was sleeping much longer, but waking up feeling tired as though energy had been taken from him, which was reminiscent of Andrew Power's experience in that room. It is worth pointing out that Lucasz had had no other paranormal experiences before coming to the Royal Oak and had been fairly sceptical about such things.

Kath Payne described a strange experience that had occurred in autumn 2012 when she was vacuuming the Poppy Room on the top storey. Her daughter Sydney (aged three and a half) was with her and started talking in a different accent to someone who was not visible. Kath picked her up, took her out of the room and asked who she was talking to. Sydney said she was talking to a man who wanted to take the baby home. After finishing vacuuming, Kath took her downstairs and went into the kitchen, where Sydney sat on the step. When Rachael's phone rang, Sydney said, 'That's the man upstairs. You're talking to the man upstairs with the baby' (Rachael was actually speaking to Andrew Power). Kath carried Sydney into the dining room and told her to look at the pictures; Sydney pointed to the one with Andrew and Rachael in it. Kath then returned with Sydney to the west bedroom to finish her work. Sydney wanted to sit in the rocking chair and said the man and baby were also sitting in the chair.

Nick and Gina Bathe reported strange experiences when they stayed in the west room: on one occasion Gina opened the bedroom door in the day and saw a shadow on her bed as she stepped into the room; she then went out and immediately came back in, but the shadow had gone. Both of them experienced the sensation of their hair being stroked and Gina also felt her legs being caressed. There was a guitar in the room and Gina recalled hearing the sound of strumming, despite the fact that Nick was fast asleep at the time.

A number of other male apparitions have been reported. A much respected customer, now deceased, recalled to me how he had seen the ghost of local quarryman Les Harris in the summer of 2010 while sitting in the bar having his tea. Les appeared to be leaning against the wall by the passage and watching him. He told me he had seen Les (who was a remarkably large man and so quite distinctive) when he was a child and thought he had died in the late 1960s. It is not known whether Les ever visited the pub, but he was related to Ken Harris, who had lived in the cottage next door to the pub. Martin Egan described how the first night he stayed in the pub, he saw his brother in the corner of the east bedroom on the second floor. His brother, who had died 8 years previously, appeared dressed as a hippy with long hair (he had been a hippy-type artist in life).

Barmaid Lil Hosegood described seeing a man with red hair, a ginger-red beard and a round podgy face in the pool room; the odd feature of this was that he seemed to be sitting in a strange position as though the floor was 2 ft lower. Several mediums have also picked up other figures: Angie Harrison-Page told me she had seen the figure of a sailor in a high-collared jacket behind the bar; Rachael was present at the time, but did not see him. Terri Powell described a man she had seen dressed in soldier's uniform and had a particularly vivid impression of a man in the dining room paying out money in brown packets to various men and women; she also saw the ghost of a boy in the pool room area where there would have been stables at one time, a man in the cellar, whose name she thinks was 'Jack', a man at a writing desk in the east bedroom and a man she described as 'grumpy' in the sitting room.

# Shadow Figures

Gina Bathe had a very frightening experience one evening in July 2012 involving a shadowy figure when she was lying down in the Poppy Room. She had fallen asleep while it was still light and then awoken to find the room dark and a figure moving around. She said she felt her left arm was restrained and the figure appeared to be trying to stick something into it. Gina was aware of the smell of damp and straw and with her right hand could feel a sack-like sheet covering her. An outside light came on and illuminated the room slightly, but Gina was still unable to move:

'I thought if I could swing my legs off the bed, I would be able to move, but then I could not feel my legs on the bed. As I looked down my body in the light, to my horror all I could see moving were two stumps where my legs should be. As much as I tried, I could not move.'

The shadowy figure walked from one side of the bed to the other, adjusting things, for what seemed like ages. Eventually, the figure disappeared and Gina hastily grabbed her clothes and got dressed outside the room. When she went back inside, everything seemed normal, but it took Gina several hours to recover from the experience.

Other ghosts at the Royal Oak have sometimes been seen indistinctly as shadows, or through peripheral vision. It was such an experience that occurred to barmaid Laura Suttle one day in 2010 when she was behind the bar soon after it had opened not long after midday; Rachael, who was in the kitchen, was the only other person in the pub. Laura saw, out of the corner of her eye, a dark figure walk from the bar and go into the pool room. Thinking it was Rachael, she went out of the bar to follow, but there was no one there and she then discovered that Rachael was still in the kitchen. Laura described her state of mind at the time as relaxed.

Barmaid Kate Brown described how she was standing near the door to the garden one night in late January 2012 when she saw the shadow of a man standing by the entrance to the men's toilets; she said the man was very tall, but she did not get a clear impression of what he was wearing. Lucy Elford, who used to work in the pub, and Rachael both witnessed a triangular, adult-sized dark shadow moving from the dining room entrance to the pool room when they were sitting in the bar around Halloween time, 2009. Rachael also has a video (which I have seen) that shows a dark shadow appearing for a split second by a wall in the bar around 3 a.m. on 12 December 2010. One customer, Claire Richards, recalled seeing the blur of someone going past in the pub, while regular customer Peter Dyke, who described himself as fairly sceptical about the paranormal, related to me how one evening in early 2011 he saw a shadow in the mirror by the front door as he picked up his coat to leave the pub soon after 11 p.m. When he turned round, there was nothing there to account for it and he found the experience unnerving.

# Glasses and Bottles

Jsanine Jenkin's experience with the moving glass has already been related, and there have been others since. Both Lil Hosegood and Jan Poole witnessed a half-pint Guinness glass shatter in the pub: the glass was on the counter and had been there for about an hour when it suddenly imploded; the strange thing was that the bottom half was shattered, but the top half remained intact. Another peculiar incident with a glass occurred when Peter Dyke saw a glass smash itself on the bar floor as if someone had dropped it; Rachael confirmed to me that a large wine glass had smashed on the floor and that it could not have come from the shelf as it was too far away. A visitor to the pub had a disconcerting experience at the bar when a bottle of J2O came off the drinks stand on the counter and hit his arm before falling to the floor. He emphasised that the bottle had hit him with some force: his initial reaction was that he might have knocked it off, but he then realised that he was not near enough. Regular customer John Lloyd related how on one occasion he had been sitting at the bar when he heard a noise and then saw a bottle behind the bar rocking to and fro before straightening up, just as though someone had brushed past it.

Another strange incident involving a glass occurred to Laura Suttle around 2009/10 when she was working behind the bar soon after midday. Only Rachael and her daughter Bryony were in the pub at the time and Laura was making some squash for Bryony: she had gone round to the back and poured a small amount into a glass, and then went to the cellar to get some more squash. When she returned, the pint glass was still upright, but most of the contents were in the sink and on the draining board, just as if someone had knocked it over. Neither Bryony nor Rachael had touched it.

# Other Moving Objects

The door leading to the stairs has a net curtain over it on the stairs side. Lucy Elford, Lil Hosegood and Rachael have all had the experience of seeing the curtain lift up and then suddenly drop down, just as if someone was there behind it, when, in fact, there was no one present. In Lil's case the movement of the curtain occurred just after she had felt someone blow into her left ear, which had scared her so much that she stood up and began to shake. Other objects apart from glasses and curtains appear to move of their own volition: Claire Richards told me she has seen the lantern in the bar moving from side to side, but even more bizarre were the two experiences that Kath Payne had with pictures. The first occurred on a Friday evening in July 2011 when the picture of the young girls in the pool room was seen to rock from side to side; no one had knocked it and there were several witnesses to the bizarre movement. The second was on a Monday evening in August 2011 during a darts match when Kath was standing near the dart board in the bar marking the score and a picture moved twice. She first noticed the picture at the side shaking slightly for no apparent reason and then, shortly afterwards, it came off the wall and hit her with some force, just as if someone had thrown it, prompting Kath to jump back; several other people witnessed this. If the picture had simply fallen off the wall, it should have dropped straight down and not jumped sideways. Kath also reported several incidents during a pool game she was playing in May 2012: the red ball moved 4–6 inches of its own accord when there was no vibration on the table, and Kath said there was one pocket (the one facing the cellar) where the balls would not go down when cued on that occasion.

# Noises

Various paranormal noises have been heard at the Royal Oak. The 'landing walker' has already been mentioned in connection with Jsanine Jenkin's account. Rachael has heard the footsteps many times when the pub has been empty as well as when there have been other people in the building; she described the footsteps as being very loud and heavy, like men's work boots. Both Pete Smith (a regular customer and former lodger) and Lil Hosegood have heard the upstairs footsteps and Lil has heard the sound of barrels rolling around in the pool room. There was also the occasion when she was in the bar and heard the black door (which used to lead to the toilets) creaking as if being moved and the sound of a latch being lifted; on investigation, she found the door was shut and discovered there was no latch. Terri Powell described how she heard noises above as if a heavy object was being dragged along the floor; at the time she was doing some cleaning for Rachael and there was no one else in the pub. She also experienced the kitchen door suddenly swing open and felt she was being watched. A different kind of noise was experienced by Pete Smith when he was woken up in the night in one of the bedrooms: he heard a voice close to his cheek spluttering his name in two syllables, 'Pe-ter'.

Laura Suttle described an incident that took place in 2010 during the daytime when she was working in the pub. Terri was doing some psychic readings in the room above the dining room. At the time the pub was fairly busy and Laura was walking around the bar collecting glasses. Suddenly, there was a loud bang from the direction of the dining room; everyone in the bar heard it and Laura went to investigate. She found that a picture had come off the wall and knocked over a shove-halfpenny table, which had been standing on its side near the wall; the picture was on the floor undamaged, but the glass had shattered and was lying on the pool table. The picture was not especially heavy, so was it coincidental that the shove-halfpenny table (which was heavy) had been knocked over at the time Terri was doing psychic readings in the room above? There was an interesting sequel to this in March 2012 when Terri was doing a psychic demonstration for a group of people in the bar on a Wednesday evening: she had almost finished and was giving a message to a lady when she heard the word 'picture' in her head. She was about to ask the lady what her connection with this word was when there was a loud crash from the dining room. Once again a picture had fallen off the wall, but this time the glass had not broken. The strange thing was that the picture hook was still on the nail in the wall when it would have been expected that the nail should have dropped down with the picture; the picture was hung in such a way that it would normally have been necessary to have lifted it off the wall.

# Tactile Sensations and Psychokinetic Force

A number of people have reported the experience of having something touch them in the Royal Oak. It has already been mentioned that both Nick and Gina Bathe felt their hair being stroked when they were staying in the west bedroom. Lil Hosegood, who was doing some preparation work in the kitchen in 2009, felt her t-shirt being pulled twice. Terri Powell told me that she had experienced a tap on the shoulder between the bar and the pool room, which made her hair stand on end. When I first spoke to Nick Bathe in April 2011, he told me that he had been sceptical of some of the paranormal claims at the Royal Oak, but admitted that on the occasion of Rachael's 50th birthday in the pub, he had felt a definite force as though someone was trying to take away his glass of cider (and it was his first that evening!). Subsequent events would convince Nick that there was a lot of paranormal activity at the pub.

Baden Albin (who was staying in the middle bedroom on the second floor from May 2010 onwards) experienced being poked in the back when he was describing to a member of a paranormal team investigating phenomena at the pub how his shoes were being moved around in his bedroom. Baden, it should be noted, is a very tidy person: before going to bed, he would put his shoes together, but in the morning he would find they were apart. He would also straighten the carpet before leaving the room, but when he returned it would be rucked up.

A psychokinetic force also appeared to be at work on the dart board in the pool room on the evening of 3 August 2010. Pete Smith was playing darts and finding that they were jumping back out of the board by several feet. He said the darts had definitely gone into the board, but acted like they had hit the wire; there was, however, an interval of some seconds before the darts came out, and in one case minutes! John Lloyd found the flight of one dart some distance away by the door; he then rammed a dart into the board which, to his amazement, jumped back out again seconds later. Rachael witnessed this and an elderly man also confirmed how the darts would not stick to the board on that same occasion when he was playing a game. The date was the anniversary of when a man, who had been connected to the pub, had committed suicide. Was this more than coincidence?

# Smells

At least several people, including Lucy Elford and Lil Hosegood, have reported the smell of hay in the pub (there was a stables attached to the building many years ago). Lil has experienced it in two places: behind the bar where glasses are washed, which she described as a fresh, dry smell, and by the cellar door, which she likened to the smell of wet hay. The smell of burning has also been detected when there has been no fire. Rachael has smelt smoke on a number of occasions, mainly in the corner of the bar. Gina Bathe told me how she had fallen asleep on the sofa in the bar early one morning in January 2012 and woken up and found that despite trying to speak, no one could hear her; on looking across into the pool room, she had a vision of a scorched wall at the back as if from a fire and there was no pool table. Strangely, Kate Brown independently related that she had smelt smoke that evening, yet there was no obvious fire in the vicinity. Terri Powell has also detected a burnt smell, this time on the third floor upstairs; she described it as being like the lingering smell following a fire. On another occasion John Lloyd witnessed what appeared to be wisps of pipe smoke upstairs when no one had been smoking.

# Uncomfortable Feelings

A particularly uncomfortable feeling in the ladies' right-hand toilet has been picked up by a number of people and it is interesting that many of the women prefer to use the left-hand toilet despite the fact that the door is partially blocked. Sandra Erskine told me that she simply cannot use the right-hand cubicle. Angie Harrison-Page has felt the presence of someone around the ladies and it has already been stated that Jsanine Jenkin would get the impression of being watched outside the ladies when she was cleaning. Sudden cold feelings are frequently experienced, including by regular customer Selwyn Diment-Davies, who does not normally feel the cold, except when he appears to be experiencing paranormal phenomena.

A number of psychics have reported unpleasant sensations around the cellar door, which is just off the pool room, and when Lucy Elford worked in the pub, she said she never felt comfortable in the cellar. At least several psychics have said they believe there may be human remains buried in that area and it was also there that Mark Elford had his experiences. It was therefore interesting that Swanage dowsers Eddie and Jan Rainford, who visited the pub on 12 November 2011, said, after doing their experiments, that they believed there was a body buried beneath the cellar door. Dowsing is normally carried out with a forked hazel stick, or similar tool, for the purpose of locating water, but some dowsers believe that their instruments can be used to discover other objects by asking questions. Eddie and Jan returned with some other dowsers in January 2012 and confirmed their original belief about the cellar. Imagine my own surprise when a spooky-looking face appeared on a digital photograph I had taken of the wall next to the cellar door; some people have said that the face appears to be of a lady who either is wearing a hat or has her hair done up in a knot on the top of her head. There is an indentation in the wall where the face sometimes appears, depending on the light conditions, and if it is a trick of the light, it is still bizarre. Is it possible for a spirit/entity to manifest itself in some way through a natural feature in the wall?

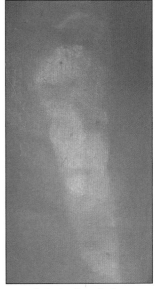

*Royal Oak ghostly face*

# The Garden

There has been considerable speculation that the Royal Oak garden may contain at least one human burial, partly as a result of the neck vertebra that was found, but also because of what psychics and mediums have said. Parts of the garden have, in fact, been dug up in recent years and in 2011 a strange stone-lined hollow was discovered, into which some 19th century beer containers had been placed. Romano-British cists (stone burial chambers) have been found in the Herston area and it is possible that an ancient cist burial may have originally been in the hollow. Mark Elford's vision of the garden from an earlier time is not the only one: both Selwyn Diment-Davies and Angie Harrison-Page feel that there was a child's grave close to the west side of the wall by the terraced area. Selwyn's most remarkable experience at the Royal Oak occurred on the night of a 50th birthday party. He had been having a conversation with Pete Smith and felt a presence, but could see nothing himself; Pete said it was Andrew Power, which would suggest some kind of astral projection. Soon afterwards, Selwyn went out into the garden and walked up the path. Artificial lights had been set up on the west side of the wall and Selwyn then experienced a vision in which he could see

*Royal Oak garden*

what appeared to be a child's grave below the wall: there was a mound of earth and a fairly small headstone and light was radiating around the grave. He could see there was something else beyond the wall and energies were radiating out from the garden. Selwyn told me that he thought intuitively the grave might have been from the early 19th century and in his vision the garden was much more level than it is now.

Angie Harrison-Page has had similar feelings to Selwyn concerning the garden. She told me that she thought there had been a child's grave in the past and that it was close to the west side of the wall by the terraced area; the child was possibly a baby and certainly no older than three or four. As we were speaking, Angie got the impression the child's grave had been that of a boy and that he had had a sister who would place wild flowers on the grave as well as something like a toy or doll. Angie, who became quite emotional, also said that the little girl had a slate and chalk and would try to talk to her brother in the grave by telling him about the animals.

What Selwyn and Angie have said about the possibility of a child's grave is especially interesting when it is remembered that Jsanine's son, Christopher, spoke to an 'imaginary friend' in the garden when he was four and later started using the word 'twin'. There would seem to be some kind of psychic link at the Royal Oak between certain people in the present and past events. Another example of this relating to the garden is what happened to Matthew Rawlings one night in 2010. Matthew was part of a paranormal investigation team and had gone into the garden to have a cigarette when he started talking to himself and listening to what he described as a kind of 'inner voice'. He was apparently standing near the spot where some ashes of a man are buried and became very emotional, describing how the man felt. Regarding Matthew, it is also of great significance that he, like Christopher, had an 'imaginary friend' around the age of three or four and had also had a twin who had died unbeknown to him; at the age of six he apparently asked if he had had a brother or sister that was missing.

Other people have experienced strange feelings at the end of the garden near to where the new wall was constructed by Andrew Power, and Rachael told me that her dog, Storm, sometimes stares at the top of the wall. Lil reported a strange incident with Storm when she had left him in the garden with his chain on and gone back into the pub. A voice then came into her head telling her that Storm was off his chain, so she went back into the garden and found that the chain was broken and Storm was standing by the steps; the odd thing was that the dog had not moved – he would normally have run off at the first opportunity.

Kath Payne described a series of bizarre experiences that had occurred to her in the late evening of 22 October 2012. She had taken Storm out into the garden and walked to the end, where she noticed the figure of a little girl sitting at the back of the gypsy caravan, which is now a permanent fixture in the garden. The girl was smiling and aged about 6 or 7, with light-coloured hair. Kath then walked over to the stone horseshoe seat, where she kept hearing a man's voice saying the words 'wood burn' or 'woodbine'. She had a very strong urge to look at the top left window (the west window on the top storey) and heard the same voice near her, saying that the pub

*Photograph of orbs taken in the garden by Lil Hosegood on the first anniversary of the death of a man associated with the pub.*

should not be changed anymore. Kath then went back inside and started to write down her experiences in Rachael's book, but could not write the word 'horseshoe' correctly, which needed three attempts. As she stood near the dart board, she heard the man's voice again and felt his presence by her shoulder. The main message seemed to be about letting him out so he would not get trapped, which, according to Kath, was connected with a fire. Rachael confirmed that there had been a major fire at the pub some years ago.

# Time Slips

As already observed, there does seem to be a strong link between the past and the present at the Royal Oak, as evidenced by the number of people reporting visions of the pub and the garden from a former time, which could be described as 'time slips', and also the numerous and varied sightings of apparitions. Rachael, too, feels that there may be a connection between herself and past events at the pub and that Andrew Power and some other people could in some way be connected. There is often the feeling when one is in the pub that time has passed very quickly; in other words, time in the pub is sometimes perceived as moving faster than in other locations. This may partly be explained by the fact that when compatible people are brought together in the same location, time will appear to speed up due to shared interests and conversation, but is there something more?

There have been several strange incidents with time pieces, one of which concerned two pocket watches that had belonged to Rachael's grandfather; bizarrely, Andrew Power became connected with both watches. One day in 2010 Andrew came downstairs with a watch he had found in a drawer upstairs (this watch had been mislaid) and said, 'Here's your grandfather's watch'. He also stated that he had 'picked up' the word 'time'. The second watch had been missing for 18 years and was found by Rachael's mother, Gill, in a family house; she gave it to Rachael, who could not open it. Terri Powell said to Rachael, 'Get Andrew to open it and pay particular attention to the time'. In February 2012 Andrew happened to be visiting and, as predicted by Terri, managed to open the watch; as he did so, Rachael saw the big hand jump back from 35 to 25 minutes past the hour.

Nick Bathe also experienced something odd with his mobile phone when he was staying on one occasion, part of which I witnessed myself. He had gone to bed at 3.20 a.m. on Monday 2 May 2011 and, on trying to set the alarm on his mobile phone, found that the phone had apparently reset itself for 13.13 on 14 March. The significance of 14 March is that it was on this very date in 2010 that Andrew Power had started to demolish the wall in the garden and, as previously stated, Andrew seems to have a strong psychic connection with the pub. When I was speaking to Nick on the Monday afternoon, the phone showed 00.48 for 15 March, but later appeared to reset itself for the correct time and date.

There was another occasion where time appeared to move backwards: on 1 May 2012 Kath Payne and another customer were looking at dates for the pool league fixtures on the computer; to their amazement, the dates on the computer unaccountably moved back by 6 days, which could not be explained as a technical glitch.

# A Case of Possession?

Linda Kelly was part of a paranormal investigations group that visited the pub in 2010 and had an unnerving time. Her most bizarre experience that evening occurred in the dining room, where she found herself having a conversation with an 'old lady' sitting behind a table in the north-east corner of the room. The lady was very old and grey with whitish hair. Linda told me that she had felt as if she were in a 'bubble' and was oblivious to what was going on around her. She had then started crying in pain, with tears streaming down her face, as she felt her arm being transferred to the lady's arm. Linda's arm was actually about an inch off the table, although she felt that it was resting on it; her hand seemed to have become stiff with arthritis, like that of the old lady, hence the pain.

# Some Observations

When considering the paranormal phenomena at the Royal Oak, three points stand out. First, the sheer number of accounts and the variety of phenomena are amazing for one location and should help to convince those of a more sceptical frame of mind. The second point is that generally the most significant experiences occur not to the spiritualists, as some might suppose, but to other people associated with the pub, such as staff and customers. Third, these people all appear to have a strong (psychic) link to the pub, which will be explored in greater detail in the concluding chapter of this book.

*Obelisk by barrow,
Ballard Down,
Swanage*

SWANAGE
WATER ACT
1888

# Chapter 4

# Near Death Experiences

There is a remarkable painting (*c* 1500) by Hieronymous Bosch known as 'The Ascent into the Empyrean' which depicts people, accompanied by angels, rising up towards a tunnel that has a bright light at the end of it. It is so unusual and seems so similar to some modern accounts of near death experiences that one wonders if Bosch drew on personal experience when painting it. For thousands of years men and women have pondered the question 'What happens when we die?' All ancient civilisations had a belief in life beyond the grave, as can be seen from archaeological finds, clay tablets, hieroglyphics and early manuscripts. In the Purbeck Hills four Bronze Age barrows were found to contain skeletons that show evidence of the bodies being trussed up before burial, perhaps to prevent the ghost from walking or to indicate a belief in life after death, with the body tied in a foetal position to symbolise new birth. The granite obelisk on Ballard Down above Ulwell stands on one such barrow and the trussed skeleton of a tall man was found at the surprising depth of 14 ft, suggesting that he was of some importance.

There are now thousands of documented cases of people who have 'returned from the dead' to tell their tales; such cases are often called 'near death experiences' (NDEs). I use this term throughout the book, but it should be noted that it is not strictly accurate as many of the people who have had such an experience suffered cardiac arrest and, according to the criteria of clinical death (which is synonymous with cardiac arrest), were actually 'dead' rather than 'near death'; in other words, their hearts had stopped beating, their lungs were no longer working and there was no measurable brain activity.

The term was coined by Dr Raymond Moody in his pioneering book *Life After Life*, published in 1975, in which he set out to show that some people (based at the time on a few hundred case studies) reported remarkable experiences when they were technically 'dead'. Since then, Dr Moody and others have documented thousands of cases and it would seem that the phenomenon is more widespread than originally thought. Those who have had an NDE report at least some of the following: a sense of being dead, peace and painlessness, separation from the body, entering a tunnel or dark region, rising rapidly into 'the heavens', meeting deceased relatives and friends bathed in light, encountering a supreme being, a review of one's life, and an unwillingness to return to the body. The core elements of an

NDE are the same whether or not the person has a religious background, though the experience may sometimes be interpreted according to the person's belief system. It should also be emphasised that many who have had an NDE say that their lives have been fundamentally transformed and a number speak about the interconnectedness of all things.

Some people report that time appears to be altered during an NDE. In a remarkable case described by Dr Moody in *Reflections on Life After Life*, a man who was trapped in an explosion and fire seemed to float above his body and saw others running to rescue him. His physical surroundings disappeared and he then had a review of his life with a 'Christ'-like figure, which in a temporal sense seemed to last at least an hour. He was told he must return and when he saw his physical surroundings again, the people who had come to rescue him seemed frozen in time. As he returned to his body, the action speeded up again. This is an especially interesting case and more will be said on the concept of time in the next chapter.

So if someone has undergone cardiac arrest and then has an NDE, which part of that person is undergoing the experience? How can people have NDEs when there is no measurable brain activity and in some cases later report accurately what medical staff were saying around their apparently lifeless bodies? Is this not an argument for suggesting that consciousness is separate from the physical brain and could survive the death of the body? Some eminent neuroscientists, including Dr Peter Fenwick, who is part of the Human Consciousness Project (an international consortium of multidisciplinary scientists and physicians set up to investigate the nature of consciousness and its relationship with the brain), claim that NDEs suggest that consciousness may indeed be separate from the physical brain.

Our understanding of what death is may be fundamentally wrong. It is sometimes possible to resuscitate a person for up to an hour following cardiac arrest, which shows that death is not a fixed point but a reversible process. At least 10–20% of people who have undergone a period of reversible death report some memories from that time, so there are a number of questions that scientists need to answer. First, if death does not happen at a fixed point when the heart, lungs and brain cease functioning, when does it occur? Second, cell death begins as soon as the heart stops beating because of the effects of lack of oxygen, but how many cells would have to die to make the process of death irreversible? Third, if our mind or consciousness can function after cardiac arrest, how long does it continue for? Lastly, why do 80% or more of successfully resuscitated patients not report NDEs?

Some sceptics have argued that NDEs may be caused by oxygen

starvation or mind-altering drugs which lead to hallucinations, but neither of these arguments stand up to scrutiny. In the case of oxygen deprivation, mental and physical abilities become progressively impaired, whereas NDEs are lucid, consistent and often life changing. Hallucinations require some electrical activity in the brain in order to occur and can be measured on an electroencephalogram (EEG), but there are many cases of people with flat EEG readings who have had NDEs. It is possible that an EEG may not record very low brain activity, but the clarity and richness of NDEs are hardly consistent with a concept of 'very low activity'. Those who attribute NDEs to the brain adopting a survival strategy when faced with a life-threatening situation cannot explain those cases where people undergoing NDEs have apparently left the resuscitation room and observed relatives in other parts of the hospital, later reporting accurately what they were doing and what was being said. There are also a few cases where a deceased relative has been encountered by the person undergoing the NDE who at the time was unaware that the relative had died! Perhaps one of the strongest arguments for the validity of NDEs is the fact that young children, who are generally free from social conditioning, also have them and report the same elements.

# Local Experiences

## Helen MccGwire

Helen MccGwire from Swanage wrote to tell me of an experience she had had in 1951 when she was returning from Australia aboard a passenger ship:

'I got measles and was being looked after in the sick bay by a nurse and one of the passengers who was a doctor, and the captain of the ship was there too. My temperature rose to 105 degrees. Slowly I found myself wafting upwards and looking down at these three people. I then looked upwards to the entrance of a long white tunnel, at the end of which was a very bright light. I felt very content and comfortable, but soon I had drifted down to my bed again. My temperature lowered and I got better, but the passengers and crew were in quarantine for a couple of weeks.'

During the experience she felt as light as a feather and as if she were made up of something like a cobweb. She was not told if she had stopped breathing or whether her heart had stopped at any stage.

## Karen Purkis

Karen Purkis used to live in Studland and spoke to me in January 2012 about an NDE she had had 2 years previously when she was seriously ill.

She had been admitted to an isolation ward at Poole Hospital suffering from swine flu and pneumonia and her blood count was down. During this anxious time, she had the experience of finding herself in a dark tunnel, with light at the end. A voice suddenly said, 'Are you ready to come?' She replied, 'No, I've got too many children.' The tunnel then closed.

## J.B. Phillips

Swanage resident Mary Eastman recounted an experience relating to Canon J.B. Phillips, who used to live in Swanage; she had been told this story by Phillips' wife, Vera, and it appears to be a classic example of an NDE.

As a young man, Phillips had a very serious illness and one night his life appeared to be in the balance. That night he had a dream in which he was standing on a bridge, but could not cross over as the way was being blocked by a being in white: this being said to him that he had to go back as it was not his time. The next morning he told his wife about the dream, by which time the crisis had passed, and he added that he would never feel afraid of death.

## John Burt

The following account was sent to me by John Burt who lives in Corfe Castle. John had an NDE after his heart stopped beating following open heart surgery. The experience convinced John that one has a soul independent of the body and that there is life after death:

'In my case the event occurred in Harefield Hospital. I had the operation for the replacement of cardiac arteries by veins from my legs and had been moved into the Intensive Care Ward for recovery. After this operation, wires are inserted into the heart muscle in case failure occurs. The heart action is monitored on an audible loud speaker which gives the familiar bleeping sound.

At this stage I was much sedated and completely unconscious, and then I became quite awake and alert and could hear a continuous audible sound which indicated that my heart had stopped beating. I could see quite clearly upwards and two men came across to me and I could hear them talking but can't remember what they were saying. I then felt electric shocks, via the wires I must presume, and it took quite a number of these but after a few faltering starts the familiar bleeps started again. With that I faded away into complete unconsciousness.'

John's brother-in-law had a similar experience in Guys Hospital when, after a similar operation, his heart also stopped beating. In his case he found himself looking down from the ceiling at the people getting his heart to beat again.

## Eddie Rainford

Swanage resident Eddie Rainford described an NDE he had had in Kenya in 1952/3 during an operation on his ear. He found himself in a tunnel with white light at the end, which was getting brighter. He then heard the words, 'Eddie, come back' and experienced a strong rushing noise, whereupon he was back in his body.

## Pete Smith

Pete Smith, who lives in Swanage, had an out-of-the-body experience when he was about 15. It occurred when he was sitting on his bed meditating and slowing his breathing and heartbeat. Suddenly, he found he was looking down on himself from the ceiling in the corner. Everything then went black, despite a light bulb being on, and Pete came to with a loud intake of breath.

# Chapter 5

# Precognition, Time and Synchronicities

Is it possible to look into the future before it happens? Certain experiments have suggested that we can, on occasion, have glimpses of the future and this challenges our understanding of what time is. Even more important are the many documented cases of premonitions and precognitive dreams that refer to real events. There is also the question of whether the future is written in stone, or if prior knowledge of it can alter or modify events; in other words, is future time a series of fixed points along a line, or can it be in a state of flux?

First, we should remember that our everyday concept of time is relative to the observer and varies according to how fast we move. Travelling fast has the effect of slowing down time, so that a clock placed at the Equator will lose time very slightly compared with a clock at the poles, because the Equator is spinning faster. A spaceship travelling from Earth to the centre of the Milky Way galaxy at nearly the speed of light (186,000 miles/second) would, for an observer on Earth, take about 30,000 years (the distance in light years from the Earth). However, those on board the ship would have aged a mere 21 years due to the effects of the slowing of time as a result of their fast rate of travel. Time has the properties (dimensions?) of duration, speed and direction and these are closely connected. It is also important to remember that whenever we observe the physical universe, we are always looking back into the past due to the time that the light has taken to reach us: we see the Sun as it was 8 minutes ago and the Dog Star (Sirius A) as it was 8.6 years ago (the time it has taken the light to reach us from those bodies). We can observe distant stars and galaxies where the light has taken many millions of years to reach us, but there is no way of knowing at that moment whether they still exist. 'Present' time in this sense has little meaning, and future time even less.

Our whole concept of time may be fundamentally wrong at a deeper level, as shown by the frequency of precognitive dreams and premonitions. Brian White from Poole wrote to me with an account of an experience he had had as a boy during the Second World War when some American soldiers announced they would give a demonstration of the game of baseball at the local recreation ground. Brian had decided to go with some friends, but on the morning he awoke in a cold sweat with the thought that he was going to be hit in the eye by a ball. He tried to get out of attending the game, but felt unable to tell his friends the reason why, so reluctantly went along as arranged. He described how during the game he spent the whole time cowering behind a friend, too petrified to even watch. Suddenly, his friend shouted, 'Look out!' and ducked: the ball hit Brian in the eye, causing it to bleed profusely, though no serious damage was done. In his letter to me he wondered whether the ball would have hit him in the eye if he had sat beside his friend rather than behind him. Would he have avoided his fate, or would, perhaps, the accident have been more serious? His foreknowledge seems to have been a classic example of a precognitive dream and in this case knowledge of the future event seemed unable to prevent it, or its consequences, perhaps because he did not heed the warning and still went to the match. There are other cases where people have avoided disasters as a result of premonitions or precognitive dreams, for example people who felt forewarned not to board the *Titanic*. This suggests that although the future event was fixed, it was possible to avoid the potential personal consequence.

If premonitions and precognitive dreams are valid (and the evidence is overwhelming), what does this suggest about our concept of time? In our everyday lives we tend to think of time as progressing in a linear way, but it would seem that this is not strictly correct. What about those occasions when an image of someone flashes into your mind when you are in the street (perhaps someone you have not seen for a while), then walking on you bump into them. 'I was only just thinking of you!', you remark. Or when someone is on your mind and the phone rings and it is that very person? 'Were your ears burning?' you might say. It seems as if time has jumped ahead of itself by a few seconds: you have perceived the meeting or phone call slightly ahead of it actually happening. Is there a sense in which time does not really exist? Mystics and those who practise meditation speak about a feeling of timelessness in their experiences when they glimpse a wider perspective; these experiences seem beyond words and the rational mind, and time, as we normally understand it, has little meaning. Our concept of time must therefore be widened to take account of all these experiences.

The future may conceivably be mapped out like a vast neural network, within which there are pathways that represent possible choices inside an overall predetermined whole. If we can speak about accessing the future through 'time slips', then this equally applies to the past, and there are examples of people who seem to find themselves in a past time situation, as noted in Chapter 3 on time slips at the Royal Oak. Can we then potentially access all time? It may be that our subconscious or intuitive mind can tune in to certain events, by using the right wavelengths, from a wider perspective of time and can form a link with other minds at a subconscious level. More will be said about this when the phenomena known as synchronicities are discussed, but now we will look at some accounts of premonitions and precognitive dreams from various people in Purbeck. First is a remarkable experience where a whole family appeared to go back in time.

# Local Experiences

## A time-warp experience

Cherry Stearn, long-term resident of Purbeck, once had a bizarre experience in which she, her children and mother all appeared to be transported back in time. It occurred on the Spring Bank Holiday in 1979 when her mother came to stay. Cherry had given some thought to where she could take her mother and had even consulted a friend, who suggested Moreton Gardens as her mother liked plants, so they and Cherry's three young children set off for what they expected would be a great day out.

When they arrived, however, they were greatly disappointed. The gardens appeared very neglected, with pathetic-looking rhododendrons covered with nettles and a path that was almost unrecognisable. Cherry noticed an old-fashioned breed of chickens and a two-planked bridge with a rope by it. Her mother was not at all impressed and they decided to wander through the gardens to the greenhouse to have a look at the plants there. Before they crossed the bridge, Cherry looked to the left and saw a couple of people scything reeds. When they entered the greenhouse, they were horrified to find six dead foxes hanging by their brushes. They lost no time in getting out of the gardens and back to the car.

Cherry's mother, who was normally sceptical of paranormal experiences, said, 'I think we must have slipped into a time warp'. Later that day Cherry phoned the friend who had recommended Moreton Gardens and said how disappointed they had been with it. 'But it's not like that', her friend responded. 'Let's go together next week.' When Cherry returned the following week with her friend, she found everything had changed and the garden looked immaculate: there were no nettles among the healthy rhododendrons, the bridge had a hand rail instead of the rope and there was no sign of any dead foxes in the greenhouse!

When I spoke to Cherry, she was clear that it would not have been physically possible for the garden to have been transformed in so short a time, or for the rhododendrons to have grown so vigorously. She is certain that somehow they had gone back to a former time.

# The ceiling collapsed

The following account was sent to me by Joy Leaton from Wareham. An interesting question to consider is the 'voice in her head': was it a presence/entity/guardian angel, or her intuitive mind? Either way, it was a timely warning to take evasive action:

'My first experience occurred when I was around 17 or 18 years old. We had had snow, the fine, dusty snow that swirls around in the air and had obviously blown into the attic of our house. It is a cold house at the best of times, but it was a particularly cold night. I had gone to bed and was cosily snuggled under my electric blanket (a luxury indeed in an old house like that). I would say that I was just drifting off to sleep when I became aware of a voice. It was a voice that I heard in my head rather than in my ears. It was nagging at me: 'Turn over. Turn over. Turn over.' I remember thinking to myself, 'Not likely, I'm too cosy and comfortable'. However, the voice persisted, 'Turn over. Turn over'. Eventually, I said aloud, 'Oh, for God's sake' (or words to that effect) and I turned over.

At the exact moment that I moved, there was a very loud crash as the ceiling collapsed. I jumped out of bed and switched on the light. I could see a clear indentation where my head had been on the pillow in which there was a large, thick chunk of plaster. I can only assume that the presence that 'spoke' to me was there to help me as I am sure that I would have sustained quite a substantial blow to the head had I not moved at the moment that I did.'

# A dream about death

Joy also experienced a dream about her great aunt's death which proved to be true.

'Another odd experience occurred on the night my great aunt died. She lived at Corfe Castle and had been bedridden for decades. My father always said that she took to her bed when he was himself just a child. We were unaware of her being ill or that her death was imminent, but she was, of course, elderly.

On this night I had a dream that I was sitting beside her bed and holding her hand. In my dream, I was aware that she was dying and sat with her until she passed away. When I believed that she had gone, I squeezed her hand to say goodbye and that was the end of the dream.

The next morning, I woke up as my mum came into my bedroom to tell me the news and I absolutely knew what she was going to tell me as soon as she opened the door. I only wish now that I'd told her before she told me!'

This is another very interesting experience. Was Joy in some sense with her great aunt when she died? Did she somehow project herself into the old lady's bedroom, or was the image of her great aunt a crisis/post-mortem apparition? Was it a dream about the present, or what was about to happen? Did her subconscious (higher self) move forward in time to anticipate what her mother would say when she came into the bedroom and then construct an image? Perhaps it is a combination of several factors. Whatever the explanation, it is a memory to treasure.

## His father's last word

A former Swanage resident gave me the following account concerning a dream he had had about his father. There are similarities with Joy's dream above.

The dream occurred in about 2000 and he had not seen his father for some time. The most significant thing in the dream was that his father called him 'son', which he did not normally do. There was a phone call early in the morning and he said he knew what it was going to be: the call was to say that his father had died.

## Warnings about accidents and death

Swanage medium Terri Powell has had a number of premonitions and precognitive dreams. A particularly significant dream occurred in about 2008 and concerned her mother-in-law who had died 2–3 years previously. This lady's sister, it should be noted, had had cancer, but had been given the all clear. In the dream, her mother-in-law was sitting on a wall waiting for Terri and she told her that her sister had got the cancer back. Terri then found herself in her old home and could see her mother-in-law's sister with her blood cells exposed. This dream proved to be a warning because months later the cancer returned and the lady died.

On two occasions Terri had a strong urge to see her grandfather shortly before he had an accident; on the last occasion the feeling apparently disappeared just as the accident happened, although she did not know this until afterwards. On the day of her grandfather's death (he was in hospital) she experienced an agitated feeling in the car of wanting to get to him, and as the feeling disappeared, she knew he had died, which proved to be the case. An even more dramatic example occurred one evening: she was coming home to Sandford on a bus with two friends and got off the bus with one of them, with both of them waving good bye to the other. The two of them then decided to go out that evening, but such a feeling of dread came over Terri that she had to leave her friend and return home early, knowing that something awful would happen. On arriving back she checked that everyone was all right at home, pacing the floor with worry, but nothing seemed amiss and the feeling went. In the morning, the friend she had left the previous evening, who lived nearby, called out to her, 'I don't want to speak to you again'; Terri was mystified until her friend explained that the third person they had left behind on the bus had been killed in a car accident that evening, so Terri's premonition had come true. 'Oh my God, what time was this?' asked Terri. Her friend then told her when it had happened and it turned out it was about the time that Terri's feeling of dread had disappeared.

## Ferry disaster

Pete Smith from Swanage had a precogitive dream related to the *Herald of Free Enterprise* ferry disaster in March 1987, which killed nearly 200 people. In Pete's dream, which took place some days before the actual disaster, a yacht called *Free Enterprise* capsized and snapped its mast; five crew members died.

While some of the details of this are obviously very different from the real disaster, the very similar name is significant. Was Pete's dream related to the actual disaster, or did he precognitively see an account of it on television or in a newspaper, which was then mixed with other elements?

## A remarkable cat

Former Studland resident Karen Purkis has sometimes had visions or dreams that came true. One of them relates to their Burmese cat, which had a very serious accident in which it nearly died. Despite the injuries, Karen insisted that the cat would recover, as she could see it in her mind playing with their daughter Portia at a later time. In fact, the cat was brain damaged for about a year and then did recover as she had foreseen; there now seems to be a close bond between the cat and Portia.

## Precognition of newspaper reports

Reg Saville's mother Beatrice, who lived in Langton Matravers, had two precognitive experiences concerning the *Daily Telegraph* newspaper, which was delivered to the house each week day. Reg describes them:

'On one occasion in 1951 she felt compelled to open it immediately it came and turn to a certain page, where she read that my brother David had been involved in a motorcycle accident on Bodmin Moor. He was doing his National Service at the time in the Royal Navy. He had kept the accident strictly to himself, so that she would not be worried.

On another occasion in August 1948 she felt compelled to look through the Births, Marriages and Deaths column in the paper. She read: 'Saville–Miles on August 7th 1948 at St Mary's Church, Guildford, Reginald John Saville married Eva Miles.' She immediately wrote to me (I was living at Harrow at the time) and asked if there was anything she should be told. It was, of course, a namesake.'

## Warning to a workman

A young lady who lives in Swanage, referred to here as 'Kate', has had a number of instances of déjà vu/precognition and believes they started after an attack of meningitis at the age of 11.

One notable example occurred when she was 13 and visiting family in Billingshurst, West Sussex. Renovation work was being carried out at the property and Kate remembers shouting out to the workman in the next room, 'Watch out for the nail', just seconds before he stepped on it.

## A ouija board's message

Linda Kelly, who lives in Swanage, has had a number of paranormal experiences. At the age of 17 Linda was using the ouija board when it spelled out a number of words that were later to prove significant: the words 'green Datsun Cherry car' came out, as did 'blond-haired husband' and 'baby boy'. About 3 years later, she was in a green Datsun Cherry car that had an accident, where she came close to being killed. She later married a man with blond hair and they had a baby boy, despite the fact that she had been told they could not have children.

This may be an example of Linda's intuitive mind jumping ahead in time by using the ouija board. There is some evidence that the use of the ouija board may be manipulated by certain entities, and it can prove scary whatever the truth; I would therefore not recommend using it.

# Synchronicities

The word 'synchronicity' was coined by the famous psychoanalyst Carl Jung to refer to those situations where simple coincidence does not seem adequate to explain several events that appear connected in an unusual way. One of Jung's favourite examples of synchronicity concerned a patient of his who was describing a dream about a golden scarab when suddenly there was a tapping noise at the window; it turned out to be a Common Rose Chafer, which is a beetle from the Scarabaeidae family. It would seem that some synchronicities are related to precognition and telepathy and are therefore bound up with time. Jung's patient may have foreseen the beetle tapping at the window through her dream and it could therefore be an example of a precognitive dream. On the other hand, was there some other principle at work that drew the two strands together?

The clearest example of synchronicity I have come across was sent to me by Stuart Sims who lives in Bournemouth. At school in Stilton, Cambridgeshire, Stuart became best friends with Malcolm, despite differences in personality. Malcolm later went to live in South Africa and the friends' final contact was in 1970. In the early 1980s Stuart and his wife moved to Bournemouth, where they ran a photographic shop. Stuart now takes up the story:

'At Easter 1996, spending time at Huntingdon with my wife's parents, I decided to go and have a look at my old school 10 miles away. Having lived 12 years at Stilton, just along the A1 from there, and having friends in the village too, only later did I wonder what was so compelling about the sudden urge to visit the old school. I was surprised to see that the post-war prefabricated building that housed my last class there had been demolished down to the concrete slab. I took a photograph of the slab as it showed the outline of the former classrooms and we returned to Bournemouth later that day.

In the summer of 1997, during a large order I was processing in my darkroom, that photo I had taken of my school the previous year that I'd never printed came into mind, so, despite being pressed for time, I looked out the negative and printed a copy. That evening Malcolm phoned from London (the first contact for 27 years!). He said how he had been in the UK the previous year and had tried to find us, but we had moved from near Peterborough to Stilton, then to Bournemouth since he last saw us; however, he did find someone who said we had moved here, but by then he had to return to South Africa. He had just arrived from there again, so the first thing he did on his arrival was to start phoning the 'Sims' in Bournemouth and got us straight away. He told me how our old school was no more and that during his search for us the previous year he had dropped in there to have a look. He and I had looked at the place on the same day, just 2 hours apart and 40 years after we were last there together! He had flown into the UK this time passing over Bournemouth at the time I decided to print that picture earlier that same day. Given the timescales involved, I find it difficult to believe these connected events are mere coincidence.'

In fact, the mathematical probability of these events being attributable to 'mere coincidence' must be huge. It was clear from Stuart's letter that he and Malcolm had had a close rapport as boys and that this continued into adulthood, so it would seem that this amazing synchronicity was constructed at a subconscious level through a telepathic link between two minds. The time is also important here: they both visited the school site on the same day and Stuart decided to develop the photo a year later around the time that Malcolm's plane was flying over Bournemouth. This example shows the hidden potential of our subconscious mind.

## Two synchronicities related to location

Swanage resident Phil Murray described two strange synchronicities that have stuck in his memory. The first occurred in 1966 on an Easter school trip to Paris when Phil was at the top of the Eiffel Tower with a friend. They wanted someone to take a photograph of them and noticed a couple standing a few yards away with their backs to them, so Phil went up and said, 'Excuse me'. When they turned round, Phil was astonished to see that he knew the couple, as they were from the same village of Ash Vale in Surrey as himself!

The second occasion was in September 2009 when Phil and his wife Mo were staying in the small Italian town of Tropea (population 6,000–7,000) in a remote area of Calabria. Their hotel was situated about 2 miles from the centre and, as there was very little public transport, they decided one morning to take the hotel minibus to the centre to look at the market and do some sightseeing. Phil described how they were walking down one of the side roads past a small cafe when they noticed a couple sitting outside having some refreshment. Suddenly, he realised they were friends from Swanage, which was remarkable considering the location. It transpired that these friends were staying in a villa farmhouse nearby.

## In close proximity

Brian Dorey from Swanage sent me this account of how he met his future wife, Val.

'Mr Brian Dorey and the future Mrs Val Dorey first met at a party somewhere in the region of Chelsea on a Saturday in February 1974. Mr Dorey was somewhat hoarse, having been cheering and no doubt deriding in relatively quick succession the players of West Ham United during the afternoon. In conversation, the two individuals were surprised to find that they worked opposite one another at the southern end of Mark Lane, London EC3. Brian had very recently been moved to Kings Beam House, which was then the headquarters of H.M. Customs and Excise, and Val was employed in Cereal House. The road outside their two buildings was extremely narrow with one-way traffic only and the two front entrances directly facing each other were probably less than 10 yards apart. It therefore seemed very strange that in a city the size of London two people should meet only to discover that they unknowingly were within such close proximity while at work.

Brian's father, who was born and lived in Herston as a boy, travelled daily to Poole Grammar School by train, and in 1930 at the age of 16 employment beckoned. A relative living in London obtained a position for him, but owing to family circumstances he was unable to take it up. If he had done so, it would have been at Cereal House.'

## Who'd a thought it?

Swanage resident Jan Rainford described an experience she had had when she was trying to book accommodation in Glastonbury. She phoned the 'Who'd A Thought It Inn' (where they had stayed before), only to be told that there were no vacancies. She then rang what she thought was the number of a second inn, but found to her embarrassment that it was the 'Who'd A Thought It Inn' again. She started to apologise but was promptly informed that they had just had a cancellation.

This seems to be an example of telepathy or precognition, where the subconscious mind had been operating.

# Chapter 6

# UFO Sightings

The vast majority of UFO sightings probably have a natural explanation, but this still leaves a small but significant number that are much more difficult to account for. Theoretical physicist Michio Kaku (in *Physics of the Impossible*) suggests that at least 95% of reports can be attributed to natural causes, such as the planet Venus, meteors, balloons, aircraft and radar echoes. There is also the increasing problem of Chinese lanterns: Swanage estate agent and lifeboatman David Corben had an interesting sighting of two objects over Swanage Bay on 31 August 2009, but later concluded that they were Chinese lanterns and said that he has picked up the remnants of these items on a number of occasions while walking in Durlston Country Park. As a lifeboatman, David is obviously a trained observer and he described to me a more unusual sighting he had had in the late 1990s out in the Channel with three colleagues: they saw a light in the distance which they thought might be coming from a fishing boat, but suddenly it shot up vertically at great speed; none of them could account for this and David felt that no technology on Earth is currently capable of such a feat of speed.

Some of the most convincing UFO sightings, in fact, are those by trained observers and also where there are multiple witnesses. A number of commercial and military pilots have seen UFOs, with some of them tracked on radar; astronauts, too, have reported sightings on space missions, and there are scientists and military leaders who consider that some UFOs could have an extraterrestrial origin. Dave Caswell from Poole drew my attention to the UFO that was seen near Brixham, Devon, at noon on 28 April 1967; his father, who had been a pilot, was one of numerous witnesses that day, including seven coastguards, one of whom made a detailed drawing of it. Dave's father was on Broadsands Beach and looking out to sea when he saw a cylinder-shaped object hovering over Berry Head near a fenced-off government area. A report in the *Sunday Express* on 21 May in that year described how the coastguards watched for more than an hour through high-powered glasses as a giant cone-shaped object hovered 15,000 ft overhead; the object slowly revolved, revealing some kind of door in its side. An aircraft approached the object and flew round it and it is believed it was tracked by radar. Eventually, the UFO vanished behind a cloud after climbing to about 20,000 ft. Many people along the Devon coast telephoned the police about the object and the coastguards' report was forwarded to the Ministry of Defence via the RAF at Plymouth. Bizarrely, the MoD suggested that it could have been a reflection of car headlights. The Chief Officer at the coastguard station, Harry Johnson, later dismissed the MoD's reaction as 'laughable'.

The above account is especially interesting due to the number of witnesses and the fact that the coastguards were able to make detailed observations. The 'official' explanation is totally absurd. There is some evidence in other cases that government agencies have possibly attempted a cover-up, or at the least been overly dismissive. It is also interesting that there appear to be a cluster of sightings from certain areas and that sightings seem to occur in waves (1954, 1968, 1973 and 1977–79 being notable years in Britain). UFOs have been reported from all over the world, with many sightings from Britain, the United States, Russia and Brazil. In a lot of cases it may not be clear whether the object seen was a UFO, though there are sometimes good indications such as the object changing direction suddenly while moving at speed, interference with electrical instruments and a creepy feeling associated with the sighting. There is also the interesting question of whether such sightings are perceived intuitively or through the rational mind.

Are these objects evidence of visitors from another world? It is certainly possible, given the vastness of the universe and the probability of extraterrestrial life. Nick Pope, author of *Open Skies, Closed Minds*, worked for the MoD and was given the role from 1991–4 of investigating UFO reports in Britain; he came to the conclusion that a small percentage of UFOs are extraterrestrial and could pose a threat. Carl Jung favoured the idea that UFOs were psychic impressions from our collective unconscious, but that does not explain how some objects can be tracked on radar and the interference with electrical equipment. Others have argued that they may be visitors from our future travelling back in time. If there is an E.T. explanation, perhaps the majority of the craft are simply probes without any alien life on board.

Assuming for a moment that intelligent life forms have visited this planet and are monitoring it, they will have had to overcome the problem of travelling vast distances at nearly the speed of light; such aliens might be many thousands or millions of times in advance of us and would appear like gods in comparison. Some physicists rank hypothetically advanced civilisations in other parts of the universe according to three stages based on the consumption of energy; Earth has not even reached stage 1 as it has not yet mastered the use of every form of energy available on the planet. Whether or not such civilisations of advanced aliens actually exist is debatable, but the suspicion among many ufologists is that government agencies are aware that aliens are visiting this planet but have ordered a cover-up to avoid a mass panic; it is not clear what the purpose of the alleged alien visits is, and if there is any hostile intent, there is little that our technology could do to prevent it.

# Purbeck Sightings

## Red lights over Kimmeridge and Creech

One of Alf Stearn's hobbies is flying model aircraft and, when the weather conditions are suitable, he sometimes goes out with a small group of like-minded enthusiasts. In the early 1970s he had an experience that he finds difficult to explain.

It was one evening in late summer when Alf and a few others had been flying model aircraft in the Kimmeridge area close to Swyre Head. By around 9–10 o'clock, when it was quite dark, only Alf and a friend were left and they sat chatting about various projects. Suddenly, two red lights appeared from a north-easterly direction and shot straight out to sea. Alf said the lights were very close together, rather like the rear lights of a car, and kept an equal distance apart as they moved at high speed. The strange thing was that there was no detectable sound, such as would be expected from a fast moving object.

Alf's wife Cherry had a rather similar experience, which may have been in the same year, when they were living at Norden Farm. She happened to be looking out of her kitchen window towards Creech Barrow when she saw two red orbs, some distance apart, flying over the barrow and heading in a westerly direction. Cherry promptly phoned a friend who lived at Creech Bottom and was told her friend's husband had just seen the objects. He apparently contacted the Lulworth and Bovington army camps to ask if there was any military activity to account for the sightings, but was told that there was not.

## A creepy feeling

Judy Clegg from Swanage sent me this account of a sighting which took place in about 2000:

'I was looking at stars in my back garden late at night when I saw a really bright light overhead. It then moved to another position instantly and fairly soon disappeared [Judy later described it as a dematerialisation followed by a rematerialisation rather than a lightning-like movement]. I do know what satellites, helicopters, etc. look like and it was certainly none of these. What I remember most was the creepy feeling it gave me, almost as though it was watching me.

At the time, 2CR radio was asking for reports of strange sightings and I did ring to report this. I've never contacted a radio station before or since then, so I think this shows how profound an experience this was.'

## New Year's Eve 2009

Swanage resident Pete Smith described how he had seen seven orange lights (similar to street lights) in the sky on New Year's Eve 2009. At the time he was with his wife and youngest son and they were walking near the Vista Bar. Suddenly, three orange lights appeared in the sky from the north, closely followed by four more. He saw two moving off at terrific speed in one direction and another two moving off another way; the movement was too fast for aeroplanes. His wife later confirmed this and said the objects were definitely not Chinese lanterns.

Readers may consider it significant that orange lights were also seen over the Manchester/Bolton area (travelling at great speed) that same night, as well as over Germany.

## A star-like object

I am grateful to John Hayes of ufoinfo.com for allowing me to reproduce the following sighting from his website, which was made over Swanage. No name is given for the witness.

'On the evening of Monday 23 June 2008 at 11.15 p.m. I was looking out of our bedroom window to the west in Swanage, Dorset. The sky was perfectly clear. I saw what looked like two stars next to each other and one 'star' seemed to be much brighter and twinkle more than the other. Then, to my surprise, the 'twinklier' star started to move off to the north (the other star was just that because it never moved and seemed to be part of whatever constellation we can see in that part of the sky at this time of year).

I watched the object carry on travelling north and then it changed to head east over Swanage. As I was indoors, I couldn't hear if it was making a noise and it did look like it was very high in the sky. It wasn't travelling at breakneck speed, but rather at a steady, but still very quick rate. The most noticeable thing was that the whole object seemed to be comprised [sic] of a bright yellow pulsating light.'

# Chapter 7

# The Significance of the Phenomena

A point has now been reached where it is possible to attempt some analysis of the significance of the paranormal phenomena described in this book. While much will be speculative, there are a number of common elements, or patterns, that emerge when the accounts are examined as a whole and may be used as a basis to draw a few conclusions.

The first three chapters, which are mainly on the subject of ghosts and related phenomena, contain elements that occur repeatedly at different locations, and the most significant experiences are those that make a lasting impression, may be repeatable and shared by others, perhaps occur at a significant time, or seem to be detected by animals as well. First, there are the actual sightings themselves: ghosts usually seem to be experienced when we least expect them and we are therefore caught unawares; our rational mind is 'off guard'. Quite a number of witnesses spoke about seeing ghostly figures, or shadows, out of the corner of their eye (peripheral vision), such as Vickie Walters at the Quay Inn and Richard and Charlotte Rose at the Manor House Hotel. On occasions, an apparition is perceived more directly and may be mistaken for a normal person until it suddenly disappears, such as the figure that Kath Payne saw in the Royal Oak garden. Many ghosts also appear dressed in old-fashioned clothes, from the time period they would have lived in (has anyone ever heard of a naked ghost?). One question is whether ghosts are seen visually or through the mind; both may perhaps occur at different times. If a ghost is perceived through the mind, it may explain why one person will see it and others not.

Now it would seem that for ghosts to manifest themselves, some kind of energy must be involved. Energy and mass are connected in Einstein's famous equation (energy = mass × the speed of light squared) and since ghosts do not appear to have mass (at least not in any known form), they may either use their own form of energy or, more likely, utilise that of the people observing them. The fact that some ghosts appear to be fairly solid, while others are nebulous, may be an indication of different levels of energy. It is possible that after a certain period of time, a ghostly manifestation may lose most of its energy, rather like a battery running down, so that appearances become weaker until no more are experienced, which may explain why there are so few ancient ghosts. There are also examples, particularly from the Royal Oak, where various people have reported their energy being drained, almost as though the phenomenon is feeding on it.

Cold feelings are frequently experienced during ghostly encounters and some haunted buildings can register cold areas on thermometers; could these be examples of heat transfer from one source (a person or location) to some kind of entity, which needs the energy to manifest itself? The corollary of the Second Law of Thermodynamics is that heat can only be transferred from a warmer source to a colder one. A tingly feeling in the spine (akin to a cold draught?) is also sometimes reported: both Jamie Bartlett at the Scott Arms and Andrew Welch at the Anglebury House Hotel spoke of this in connection with experiencing ghosts.

Regarding energy, there does appear to be a connection between some manifestations and electricity. It is well known that ghostly phenomena can affect electrical equipment and some of the local accounts reinforce this idea. Lights going on and off were reported at a number of sites and there were also accounts of televisions, stereos and a kettle being affected. There was even the case of a blown light bulb coming on at the Quay Inn. It would also seem that on occasions electrical equipment may record phenomena. A number of strange images have been picked up on cameras and videos at the Royal Oak, with the most surprising being seen by Lucasz Domagala's wife by means of a computer video link in Poland. At the Greyhound Inn a woman's figure was seen on a CCTV camera by Jacci Pestana, and at the Ship Inn Claire Beale saw a black figure on a camera screen. Having said that, it is interesting to note that many paranormal teams use electrical equipment, though not always with much success. Is it a question of the phenomena not wanting to play ball? As with actual sightings, things seem to occur mainly when we are not expecting them; if you sit there and wait for something to happen, the chances are that it won't. A relaxed state of mind, without undue concentration, seems essential for paranormal phenomena to be experienced. It may be that the mind needs to largely empty itself of thoughts, such as when routine tasks are being carried out, or when there is no pressure to get something done. Much of the paranormal phenomena reported by pub staff occur at quiet times when there is little pressure involved in the job and therefore concentration is not excessive.

While a human mind may be an essential link for a ghost to appear, it is also apparent that animals can be aware of manifestations, perhaps sometimes even before humans. Examples were given of dogs and cats at the Royal Oak, and dogs elsewhere, such as the Castle Inn, Quay Inn and properties on the Quay at Wareham and nearby St John's Hill. There is even the case in North Street, Wareham, where a cat and parrot were aware of the same noises that the people could hear. Dogs seem to be reported more often than other animals in association with paranormal phenomena, but this may be because they are kept more frequently as pets. When it comes to sound, the hearing of dogs and cats is much more acute than humans:

our hearing range falls between 20 and 20,000 Hertz; dogs can hear up to 45,000 Hertz and cats 85,000. It is not, however, just a question of sound: in the case of the phenomena in the property on Wareham Quay, it is noteworthy that while the dog became very agitated, the cat displayed no reaction (and there was nothing apparently that was unusual about this cat).

One interesting point is whether dogs and other animals are aware of ghosts independently of humans, or whether they detect them through a person's (sometimes subconscious) reaction. Some of the evidence presented in this book suggests that animals can sense paranormal phenomena before people do (Jsanine Jenkin heard the landing walker at the Royal Oak *after* the cat began growling, Joy Leaton saw the shadow of a cavalier *after* the dog's reaction, and there are other instances where a dog or cat may have experienced something when a person was apparently not able to detect it). There will, though, undoubtedly be other occasions where a dog or another animal appears to sense something from a person's reaction.

Whether animals have some form of telepathy is also interesting to consider. Stuart Sims (who appears in the section on 'Synchronicities' in Chapter 5) told me about a dog they used to have which would alert them to impending visitors about 15 minutes before they arrived; the dog was so accurate that Stuart's wife would put the kettle on as soon as it started behaving in this way! Stuart also described how the same dog would anticipate when he was about to be taken for a walk in the evening, despite the fact that Stuart would do it at random times and there seemed to be no physical signal that the dog was picking up. The only conclusion was that the dog was somehow reading his thoughts. Likewise, Mo Murray has commented that her cats often seem to be waiting for her when she gets home, which is at different times; it is almost as if they know she is about to arrive.

It seems fairly clear that there are different types of apparitions, and one of the founders of the Society for Psychical Research, G.N.M. Tyrrell, divided them into four categories, which is a useful starting point in trying to understand the phenomena. First, many ghosts seem to fall under the 'haunting' category, where they are seen in a particular location over a period of time, and more will be said on this in a moment. Second, there are 'crisis apparitions', ghosts that appear at a time of great trauma and can be seen to be apparitions of the living, perhaps created through some telepathic link that is activated at a time of great stress (the example I gave in the Introduction of my uncle being 'seen' by my grandmother is an illustration of this). Third, there are 'post-mortem apparitions', ghosts that appear to someone (often a family member or friend) soon after their death. If hallucinations are excluded, the most likely explanation is that these could be disembodied spirits. The C.S. Lewis case in Chapter 1 is an example of this. Finally, there are cases where apparitions have been consciously and deliberately created, or projected, by a living agent. An interesting example of this was created by Alexandra David-Neel (see *Magic and Mystery in Tibet*) who, through certain rites and concentration, produced the figure of a monk, which eventually began to take on a life of its own; even more significant was the fact that a visiting herdsman saw the figure himself, though he was unaware of her experiment. It may also be possible to create ghosts subconsciously when the conditions are right.

Most of the ghosts reported in this book come under the haunting category, so what exactly are these apparitions and how are they formed? It would seem that the vast majority are echoes from the past and that certain people have the ability to tune into the right wavelength on occasions, picking up an image, a shadow, or possibly just a strange feeling through their intuitive mind. This person needs to be receptive, which means being open-minded, imaginative, relaxed and perhaps empathetic, while other conditions may also be necessary, perhaps related to meteorological or electromagnetic factors. It is also possible that the time of day may be important: quite a lot of paranormal activity seems to occur late at night (including, obviously, interesting phenomena relating to dreams) and there may be a link here with the production of the hormone melatonin (peak production is 3–6 hours after the onset of darkness) from the pineal gland, which is sometimes referred to as the 'Third Eye'. It may also be of relevance that some religious groups practise meditation and prayer in the early hours of the morning when the production of melatonin is at its highest.

As mentioned above, many of the haunting apparitions are echoes of the past and seeing one is like watching a film, where the ghost seems to be going about its business as it would have done in its life and is unaware of anyone observing it. There are, however, examples where some interaction occurs between the apparition and the observer: in the case of Lucasz Domagala's sighting of the young girl at the Royal Oak, he described how she disappeared behind one door and then another, just as if she were playing a game with him. This experience seemed to be more than just watching a film: the ghost appeared to be aware of him. Is this therefore an example of a disembodied or trapped entity, or can a haunting apparition, like an experimental one that has been created, take on a life of its own on occasions, perhaps if it is given more energy? At both the Old Granary in Wareham and the Red Lion in Swanage a number of people have reported hearing their name called, which are clearly examples of interactions. There are also the cases (the Red Lion, Swanage, and property on the Quay in Wareham) where people have woken up in the night and felt a weight on top of them and a figure, or shadow, has been seen. These examples were clearly very unwelcome interactions and much more than echoes from the past! They seem to be akin to some kind of psychic attack and there are some writers who suggest that certain entities may attempt sexual intercourse; whether this is the case or not, the best means of defence seems to be a strong will power, or perhaps prayer for those who believe in it.

Assuming there are certain people who can experience hauntings when the conditions are favourable, the question arises of how these apparitions were produced in the first place. If we accept the view that everything that has ever happened can potentially be tuned into by a sensitive person, then images/figures of everyone that has ever lived could theoretically be seen and millions of ghosts should be reported, which is clearly not the case. While very psychic people do seem to have the ability to experience far more phenomena than most, the typical apparition in hauntings is often seen by several witnesses and must be created by specific conditions. One of these factors is likely to be a strong emotional link, whether it is violent, tragic, sexual or an attachment to a specific place. In the case of some hauntings, the apparition is often of a person who was murdered, had a tragic accident, or suffered some long-term emotional stress; in others, the person may have been strongly attached to a particular room in a building. The emotional factor does appear to be a significant point: a number of psychics seem to have picked up on emotional events from the past at the Royal Oak, and one of the most interesting comments came from Mark Elford, who described the pub as having 'a trapped emotion which cannot pass'. Other stories such as the 'White Donkey' at Studland, Trent's at Langton Matravers, the 'Headless Woman' at Corfe Castle, and the Old Granary at Wareham seem to be connected with violent or tragic events. Andrew Purkis also spoke about unhappiness in the past in association with Manor Farmhouse, Studland, and in some other cases the ghost may, in life, have had a strong emotional connection with a particular location.

While emotion is obviously a key factor, it cannot be the only reason for a place to become haunted; there must be many buildings that have seen emotional events, where hauntings do not seem to take place (considering its violent history, one might have expected more activity from Corfe Castle, or has the energy run out because it has been ruined for so long without people living there?). Although the age of a building may be a factor in so far as it will have a longer history and therefore more time for emotional events and other aspects to occur, there are examples of old buildings locally where paranormal phenomena have not been reported. The specific location of a building may be more important (perhaps partly for geomagnetic reasons) and there is also the theory that there may be 'weak points' in space and time in certain places, where phenomena from one dimension can sometimes leak into another. A connection with (running) water is probable: there has been considerable paranormal activity around Wareham Quay near the River Frome and water may also be linked to the sightings at St Edward's Cottage, Norden, and possibly the Royal Oak (it is believed that a well exists there). Disturbance to a building is likely to be a contributory factor in some cases, including major renovation and a change of owners. It also seems probable that there are certain people (I call them 'catalysts') who set off or disturb the phenomena. These people may themselves be very psychic, possibly disturbed in some way, or have 'dabbled' at some point in their lives. They may have intense energy, which is unchannelled and looking for a focus. The psychic phenomena then feed on their energy and grow stronger. Some well-known poltergeist cases appear to centre around one person, often an emotionally disturbed child. It has often been noted that paranormal phenomena at different locations wax and wane: there are times when a lot seems to happen, followed by quieter periods. Could it be that these 'catalysts' act as a trigger for the phenomena and that they are like transmitters? Other people who happen to be in the right frame of mind (relaxed, imaginative, empathetic) pick up the phenomena intuitively and act as 'receivers'.

It is important to consider some of the other common elements experienced at haunted locations when apparitions are not seen. One of the most frequently reported sounds is that of footsteps and sometimes the sound of heavy objects being moved. Certain objects may be displaced and on occasions are actually seen to move (even in slow motion, as at the Anglebury House Hotel and another property in North Street, Wareham). Distinctive smells, such as perfume, tobacco and hay, have been detected. Loud noises and moving objects are frequently reported in association with poltergeist activity, but in some of the accounts there is often a link with haunted sites. The 'landing walker' heard at the Royal Oak is most likely the sound of a former workman who used to live in the pub; in this case the sound is experienced, rather than an apparition, perhaps because the sound of his heavy boots was his most characteristic feature, which may have led to extreme irritation (a strong emotion) on the part of other people living with him. What are people actually experiencing when they hear such a sound? Are they able to tune in to something that was somehow recorded in special circumstances in the past, and have they in a sense gone back in time? Or is it a question of a trapped spirit letting it be known that it is still around? It is the same question that was asked about the sightings of apparitions and I am inclined to favour the former explanation in the majority of cases because much of the activity seems mechanical, with the person experiencing it being a witness rather than interacting with it.

Another important point to consider is how time fits in with some of the phenomena experienced. At the Royal Oak, in particular, some of the witnesses seemed to be almost transported back in time where they would be seeing a snapshot of the past, in connection with not only some of the rooms inside but also the garden at the back. Did they in a sense 'travel back in time'? There is also the remarkable time warp experience of Cherry Stearn and her family when they appeared to see Moreton Gardens as they might have been in a former time. As was noted in Chapter 5, some people also seem to have the ability on occasions to catch glimpses of the future and in a sense travel forward in time. The evidence from precognitive dreams and premonitions seems to suggest that our everyday notion of time is very limited and is certainly unsatisfactory to explain many complex things in life. If, at a deeper level, there can be a transcendent awareness of both past and potential future events, then our concept of linear time is fundamentally wrong. Does time really exist if it is sometimes possible to access the past and also the future? It is interesting that in the case of the phenomena at the Anglebury House Hotel (the milk going back into the container) and a nearby property in North Street, Wareham (the plate falling), both were observed in slow motion, almost as though time had slowed down. In some NDEs, people report that time appears to be altered: the review of one's life, which, in a linear sense, would require some period of time, seems to occur almost in a flash. There could, therefore, be some kind of 'eternal' time where the linear concept of past, present and future merge, which our higher self can occasionally catch glimpses of when we are not absorbed in our everyday, more mundane affairs. This, in turn, suggests a kind of 'information universe' (an expression coined by paranormal writer Colin Wilson) that can be accessed subconsciously by our intuitive mind. I think that in order for this to happen, there must be a link between ourselves and what is being accessed in the past or future. John Dunne (1875–1949) was an aircraft designer and also noted for his famous theory of time. It is noteworthy that some of his dramatic precognitive dreams, such as the volcanic eruption on Martinique, were related, not to the actual future event itself, but to his reading about the future event; in other words, Dunne's psychic link was to the future newspaper account he would read. Many such dreams and also premonitions will, if examined carefully, reveal evidence of a link between the person and what is going to, or may, happen. Those who have dreamed about future disasters are often connected in some way, perhaps because they, or their relatives, were planning to be there at the time, or they would subsequently see news coverage of the event if it were of major importance. I could be wrong, but I think it is unlikely that premonitions and precognitive dreams are related to events that are not linked in some way to the person experiencing them.

Some kind of psychic link may also be necessary in the case of 'time slips' in the past, where people have the ability to see a snapshot of history, like watching a film. What, then, is the link between these people and the past? Were they somehow connected to past events? It is perhaps no coincidence that some of the most remarkable experiences at the Royal Oak have occurred to people who seem most connected with the pub: Mark Elford, Andrew Power, Gina Bathe and Selwyn Diment-Davies have all had experiences related to time displacements, while others such as Kath Payne, Lil Hosegood and Jsanine Jenkin have had multiple experiences, where they seem to have accessed something from the past history of the building, whether it is a ghost, a sound or a smell. Some may wish to maintain that these people were all connected to the pub in a previous incarnation, which, while it may be true, could never be proved, but what is indisputable is that they all have a strong emotional link to it now, and emotion, as has been argued, is a key factor in creating paranormal phenomena.

If, as has been proposed in this book, our intuitive mind can perceive certain paranormal phenomena, such as apparitions, poltergeist activity, telepathy and precognition, our rational mind is equally necessary to make sense of what we experience and to formulate theories (the problem is where the rational mind interprets an experience so as to fit it inside a narrow, pre-existing framework, as has been the case with some religious beliefs). It is therefore possible to draw a distinction between the actual experience and our thoughts about what we are experiencing. Most of us can appreciate the beauty of a wood in the spring: there is the experience itself, with its different colours, sounds and smells, which we can contemplate, drawing it into ourselves and becoming one with it; at the deepest level, a type of mystical experience may occur where our very being seems to merge with it. The appreciation of beauty does not require rational thought, but we can rationalise about the elements that make up this beauty: the wood, for instance, may be a sea of Bluebells, interspersed with Red Campion, Primroses and Wild Garlic, the latter giving off a pungent aroma, while all around the trees resonate to the mellifluous tones of Blackbirds, Song Thrushes, Robins and Willow Warblers. Our senses are being bombarded by different colours, sounds and smells and we can add a new dimension by giving names to them and explaining what they are; in other words, we can rationalise our experience. Great works of art (paintings, sculptures, musical compositions and poems) may largely be produced by the intuitive mind and at the same time appreciated intuitively; it is when we start to consciously think about what makes them great that we find it difficult to explain rationally, but it is still possible to at least make an attempt. It is probable that man's rational side has grown to keep pace with the increasing demands of modern civilisation, but there have also been opportunities for the intuitive side to evolve as well where the arts have flourished.

What is termed 'consciousness' is most likely a combination of the intuitive and the rational (our experience and our awareness of it) and it would seem from the evidence presented in Chapter 4 that some part of this survives bodily death. Does consciousness itself have some form of energy, I wonder? Anyone who makes a study of NDEs will soon be able to see the pattern of common elements described earlier. It is my view that NDEs offer the best evidence for survival of consciousness beyond death of the physical body because the common elements experienced suggest an objectivity to the phenomena; the varied background of the people who have had these experiences (many without preconceived belief systems), plus the life-changing effects add to the validity. It is certain that the evidence will continue to accumulate as more studies into NDEs are made in different countries and a point will be reached where it will become so overwhelming that the majority of scientists may accept it. If, or when, that happens, it will signal an end to the materialist philosophy and the reductionist view that some scientists adopt, because a comprehensive model of consciousness will be required, one that encompasses the findings that suggest that it is, indeed, separate from the physical brain. If incontrovertible evidence (rather than belief) can be offered for survival beyond physical death in some form, our way of life will be changed forever: war, greed and selfishness will be seen to be futile and a new spiritual philosophy, based on evidence rather than pure belief, transcending all narrow religious divisions may ensue. At the same time, greater respect for our planet as well as each other will be another natural consequence. None of this will be achieved overnight, but will come through a gradual dawning of what is important in life: a realisation of long-term values rather than instant gratification.

One of the great driving forces on our planet and throughout the universe is evolution, which operates in different ways at various levels. Everything is subject to change, whether it happens to be on a small scale or something much grander, and this fact is a key point in Buddhism. Nothing is fixed in time: species change, ideas change and the universe is dynamic. If there are indeed worlds beyond the physical, then there may be some force that underlies and perhaps drives matter (whether we want to call this 'God', 'Spirit' or 'Life Force' is immaterial). Our consciousness (in the sense of our awareness of this planet and the physical universe) has expanded greatly when it comes to the rational mind, but could it be about to undergo an equally dramatic transformation intuitively? Alongside man's shallow pursuit of materialism and the modern western obsession with trivia lies a yearning for something deeper and more lasting, which is the essential message of all religions, though it has often become submerged in later doctrine, dogma and fruitless divisions. At the heart of every religion lies an esoteric core, spoken of and taught by the original teachers and experienced by mystics and some who practise meditation. The essence of this religious experience is perceived intuitively, just as paranormal phenomena are. The best elements in western and eastern traditions are complementary, not mutually exclusive, and we all need to learn from one another. We live at a time where mass communication has increased and has become instantaneous, especially with the advent of the internet. With improved education worldwide, it will not be long before there is a greater awareness of this core experience at the heart of religion, that we are all interconnected and interdependent and that this may be perceived through the intuitive mind. When this begins to happen, coupled with increasing evidence of life after death and dimensions beyond the physical (where science, religion and the paranormal begin to merge), our evolutionary development will have moved a stage further by raising our level of consciousness. The time may then be ripe for mankind as a whole to establish the first alien contact, or perhaps it will be the other way round, for it will become apparent to any advanced alien life form that mankind has at last grown up and begun to realise its full potential.

# References and Further Reading

Bede (1983) *A History of the English Church and People* (translated by Leo Sherley-Price). Penguin Books, London.

Bernard Calkin, J. (1968) *Ancient Purbeck*. Friary Press, Dorchester.

Boar, Roger and Blundell, Nigel (1996) *The World's Greatest UFO Mysteries*. Hamlyn, London.

Bohm, David (2002) *Wholeness and the Implicate Order*. Routledge, Abingdon.

Borrett, Danielle and Stewart (1989) *Wareham Rediscovered*. Amberwood Graphics, Swanage.

*Bournemouth Daily Echo* (20 May 2009) *I saw a ghost at Corfe Castle*. Steven Smith.

Calder, Nigel (2005) *Magic Universe*. Oxford University Press, Oxford.

Cooper, Ilay (2008) *Purbeck Revealed*. James Pembroke Publishing, Bath.

David-Neel, Alexandra (1971) *Magic and Mystery in Tibet*. Corgi Books, London.

*Dorset, the County Magazine* (Winter 1969) *The White Donkey*. Benjamin Pond.

Dunne, John (1938) *An Experiment with Time*. Faber and Faber, London.

Fairley, John and Welfare, Simon (1989) *Arthur C. Clarke's World of Strange Powers*. Collins, London.

Hardy, W.M. (1978) *Smuggling Days in Purbeck*. The Purbeck Press, Swanage.

Hayman, Ronald (2002) *A Life of Jung*. Bloomsbury, London.

Horizon Research Foundation, *Human Consciousness Project and Near Death Experiences*. www.horizonresearch.org.

Hutchins, John (1973) *History and Antiquities of the County of Dorset, Volume 1*. E.P. Publishing, Wakefield.

Johnson, Raynor (1958) *The Imprisoned Splendour*. Hodder and Stoughton, London.

Kaku, Michio (2006) *Parallel Worlds*. Penguin Books, London.

Kaku, Michio (2008) *Physics of the Impossible*. Allen Lane, Penguin Group, London.

Knott, Olive (1956) *Dorset Again*. Friary Press, Dorchester.

Ladle, Lilian (1994) *Wareham: A Pictorial History*. Phillimore, Chichester.

Lazarus, Richard (1993) *The Case Against Death*. Warner Books, London.

Legg, Rodney (1998) *Mysterious Dorset*. Dorset Publishing Company, Wincanton.

Lewer, David and Smale, Dennis (1994) *Swanage Past.* Phillimore, Chichester.

Moody, Raymond (1978) *Reflections on Life After Life.* Bantam Books, New York.

Moody, Raymond (1988) *The Light Beyond.* Bantam Books, New York.

Pope, Nick (1999) *Open Skies, Closed Minds.* Overlook Press, New York.

Pridham, Llewellyn (1954) *The Dorset Coastline.* The Friary Press, Dorchester.

Randles, Jenny and Hough, Peter (1993) *The Afterlife.* BCA, London.

Robins, Joyce (1991) *The World's Greatest Mysteries.* Treasure Press, London.

Roney-Dougal, Serena (1993) *Where Science and Magic Meet.* Element Books, Shaftesbury.

Sagan, Carl (1981) *Cosmos.* Book Club Associates, London.

Saville, Reginald (2001) *A Langton Smuggler.* Langton Matravers Local History and Preservation Society, Langton Matravers.

*Sunday Express* (21 May 1967) *The Brixham Sighting.*

*Swanage Times* (27 November 1926) *Swanage Family's Bereavement.*

*Swanage Times* (12 July 1967) *The roof fell in.*

Temple, Robert (1999) *The Sirius Mystery.* Arrow, Random House Group, London.

UFO sighting reports – United Kingdom: 23 June 2008, Swanage, Dorset. www.ufoinfo.com/sightings/uk.

Uhlenbroek, Charlotte (2002) *Talking with Animals.* Hodder and Stoughton, London.

Watson, Lyall (1976) *The Romeo Error.* Coronet Edition, Hodder and Stoughton, London.

Wilson, Colin (2008) *Beyond the Occult.* Watkins Publishing, London.

# Useful Websites

www.darkdorset.co.uk
www.dorsetdowsers.co.uk
www.ufoinfo.com/sightings/uk

# Godlingston Lane

It was twilight, almost evening,
The leaves were palely greening
And berries darkly gleaming
In the hedgerow down the lane.

There are footsteps close behind me,
I can feel them all around me,
The ghosts of Saxon farmers, the shouts of Danish raiders
By the Manor, in the lane.

Or am I only dreaming, in the dimming light of evening,
As I turn around to see
Only birds no longer cheeping, but flying home for sleeping
To the hedgerow in the lane?

As I walk, the shadows lengthen
And my feelings seem to strengthen.
Can I sense what once was? Has been?
Near the hedgerow in the lane.

*Written by Emily Pashley Leadbetter*
*and read out before her interment at Godlingston Cemetery, Swanage*

'Not the end — just the beginning.'

# About the Author

David Leadbetter has lived in Swanage most of his life, where he worked at a local school teaching English to foreign students and administering examinations. David has a long-term interest in natural history and conservation and has led many guided walks locally to help people with plant, bird and insect identification. Most of his travelling has been in connection with the natural world, or historical sites, and he has a passion for Africa.

David's fascination for the paranormal started as a boy when he learned about some of his family's experiences and began to read books on the subject. He has been studying the paranormal for a number of years and is particularly interested in how it connects with certain aspects of science and the metaphysical core at the heart of some religious experience. David believes that by understanding the paranormal, our insights into this world and what may lie beyond will grow.

*Paranormal Purbeck* is David's first book to be published. Anyone who has had a paranormal experience in the area is welcome to contact him by writing to 15 Prospect Crescent, Swanage, BH19 1BD (please enclose an SAE for reply) or emailing davidleadbetter@bbmax.co.uk.

# Index

# Other Roving Press Titles

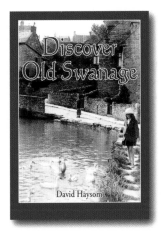

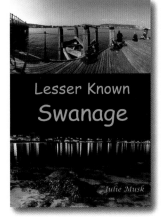

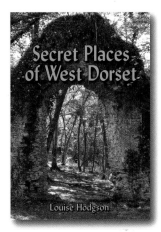

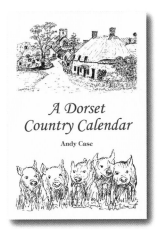

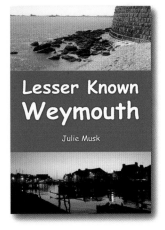

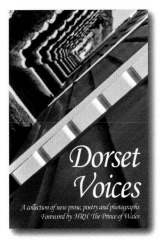

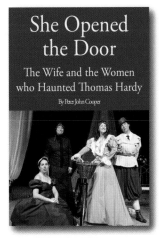

*If you like exploring, you'll love our books*

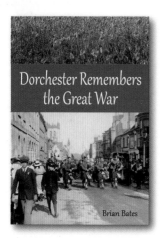

Dorchester Remembers the Great War

Brian Bates

Preston, Bowleaze and Overcombe

by D. Joan Jones

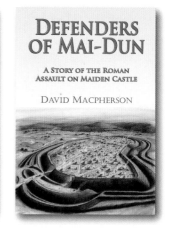

DEFENDERS OF MAI-DUN

A STORY OF THE ROMAN ASSAULT ON MAIDEN CASTLE

DAVID MACPHERSON

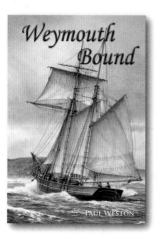

Weymouth Bound

PAUL WESTON

THE PORTLAND CHRONICLES

THE PORTLAND SEA DRAGON

CAROL HUNT

THE PORTLAND CHRONICLES

ENCHANTMENT OF THE BLACK DOG

CAROL HUNT

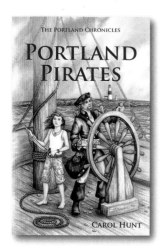

THE PORTLAND CHRONICLES

PORTLAND PIRATES

CAROL HUNT

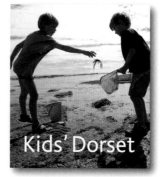

Kids' Dorset

THE PORTLAND CHRONICLES

THE PORTLAND GIANT

CAROL HUNT

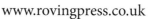

Roving Press

www.rovingpress.co.uk